MW00803386

Christ & St. Luke's

Norfolk's Landmark Church

Sigur E. Whitaker

To Karen,

Hope you will enjoy!

Sigur Whitaker

Artist's sketch of Christ & St. Luke's Church, Norfolk, Virginia in 1957

Christ & St. Luke's

Norfolk's Landmark Church

By Sigur E. Whitaker

PARKE PRESS

Norfolk • Washington

*This book is dedicated to the Glory of God
and to the memory of those Saints
who have gone before with wisdom and grace
to give us this remarkable place.*

Published by
PARKE PRESS
Norfolk, Virginia

ISBN 978-0-9883969-7-5

Library of Congress Control Number is available upon request

Printed in the United States of America

TABLE OF CONTENTS

Other books by Sigur E. Whitaker

James Allison, A Biography of the Engine Manufacturer and Indianapolis 500 Cofounder (2011)

Tony Hulman, The Man Who Saved the Indianapolis Motor Speedway (2013)

The Indy Car Wars, The 30 Year Fight for Control of Open Wheel Racing (2015)

The Indianapolis Automobile Industry: Quality, Not Quantity (2017)

FOREWORD

THE STORY OF Christ & St. Luke's Episcopal Church envelops the story of the early days of our nation, through the tumultuous times of the Revolutionary War and the Civil War, through good times and bad.

For those people who traveled by a very small boat to the shores of Virginia in 1607, the church was a mainstay and a comfort in their lives. Today, nearly 400 years later, the church, with its magnificent edifice, continues to be a beacon in times of trouble and a place in which to give thanks to God for all the blessings we enjoy.

Many people have contributed to this book. Although I had thought of doing this book from time to time, Debbie D'Angelo spurred me on to commit to undertake the effort. The Reverend Canon Irwin "Win" Lewis, Rector of Christ & St. Luke's, has been supportive and enthusiastic about the project. Kevin Kwan, Kristen Maurice, and Joel Whitaker have asked questions and have been invaluable in proofreading. Kevin Kwan, Rick Voight, Bill McIntosh and Bill Gresham have provided photos. Historic photos are from the archives of the Library of Virginia and the Sargeant Memorial Collection at Norfolk's Slover Library where Bill Inge and Troy Valos have been most helpful and enthusiastic about this project.

PROLOGUE

SEEKING A BETTER LIFE, 105 men and boys boarded three small ships—the *Susan Constant, Discovery,* and *Godspeed*—under Captain Christopher Newport in late 1606. On April 26, 1607, upon reaching the shores of Virginia after a five-month journey, they landed at what is now known as Cape Henry. Robert Hunt, a former vicar of a church in Reculver, Kent, England, was aboard the *Susan Constant.* He had been recruited by Richard Bancroft, the Archbishop of Canterbury, Rich Hakluyt, Jr., a geologist and priest, and Edward Maria Wingfield, one of four incorporators of the Virginia Company of London, as the chaplain for the expedition. Under Reverend Hunt's leadership, the adventurers came ashore, got down on their knees, and gave thanks to God for safe passage.

Seeking a more secure location from potential attack by other nations, they then re-boarded the three ships and set sail up the James River. About forty miles further inland, they found a piece of land which offered a defensible strategic point due to a curve in the river. The property was also not inhabited by the local Indians. Landing on the western shore, they established a small colony, James Fort, later renamed Jamestowne in honor of the reigning English monarch, King James I.

The settlers brought their form of government and Anglican religion with them. It is believed Reverend Hunt celebrated the first Holy Communion at Jamestowne on June 21, 1607.

Life was not easy. Although the property offered a good defense for the fort from the river, it was swampy, plagued by mosquitoes, and had brackish water that was unsuitable for drinking. Virginia was also suffering from a multi-year drought. Additionally, many of the early settlers were gentlemen, unused to the hard labor needed to establish and sustain a colony. After establishing the colony, Captain Newport returned to England to bring more provisions and additional settlers to the struggling colony. By the time Captain Newport returned with additional supplies and adventurers, about two-thirds of the original settlers had died because of starvation, disease, or conflict with the local Indians.

The colony was very dependent upon the Virginia Company of London for provisions for sustenance. The Third Supply, a convoy of eight ships bringing 500-600 people and supplies to the colony was delayed by a hurricane. When the Third Supply finally arrived in Jamestowne in May 1609, they found the remaining colonists starving. Remembering the failed colony at Roanoke, also known as the Lost Colony, the Jamestowne colony was believed by the remaining settlers to be unviable. The remaining colonists boarded the *Deliverance* and the *Patience* to return to England. As they were sailing down the James River, they encountered another supply convoy led by Baron de la Warr and returned to Jamestowne.

Investors in the Virginia Company of London wanted a return on their investment which was to come from commodities being sent from the Virginia colony back to England. They continued to send more settlers and provisions to the colony in larger ships and soon a second community, Henricus, was founded.

※ ※ ※ ※ ※ ※ ※ ※ ※ ※ ※ ※ ※ ※ ※

CHAPTER 1

The Colonial Period

B Y 1619, there were enough colonists in Virginia that a group met at the Jamestowne church "to establish one equal and uniform government over all Virginia." Thus began the House of Burgesses. At the same time, individual land ownership was instituted and the colony was divided into four large "boroughs," called "citties" by the colonists. Jamestowne was located in James Cittie. The other citties were Kecoughtan (later called Elizabeth City, now part of Hampton) founded in 1610, Henricus founded in 1611, and Charles Cittie founded in 1613.

In 1624, King James revoked the charter for the bankrupt Virginia Company of London and Virginia became a royal colony. By order of King Charles I in 1634, the colony, with a total population of 4,914 settlers, was divided into the original eight shires (counties) of Virginia—Accomack (now Northampton County), Charles Cittie (now Charles City County), Charles River (now York County), Elizabeth Cittie (now part of Hampton), Henrico (now Henrico County), James Cittie (now James City County), Warwick River (now part of Newport News) and Warrosquyoake (now Isle of Wight).

Most of the initial development in the Virginia colony occurred on the north side of the James River. Adam Thoroughgood was one of the first Englishmen to settle in south Hampton Roads. King James I also granted 500 acres to Thomas Willoughby. Willoughby's land holdings were increased when King Charles I granted him a large tract of land on the Lynnhaven River in what is now Virginia Beach. In 1636, the lands south of the James River were split off from the Elizabeth Cittie Shire, to form Norfolk County. In 1637, Norfolk County was split into Upper and Lower Norfolk County. Norfolk, Portsmouth, Virginia Beach and Chesapeake were in Lower Norfolk County while Upper Norfolk County consisted primarily of what is today Suffolk. The boundaries of the parishes were established by the General Assembly. It was also in 1637 that the Elizabeth River Parish was formed.

The parish system was also implemented by the colonial settlers. Brought from England, this system combined both governmental and religious functions. In 1641-1642, the General Assembly formally established Vestries throughout Virginia and charged the Vestries with establishing the annual parish levy. It is believed by many historians that this simply codified what had been occurring earlier. In England in 1598, "select Vestries" were established to differentiate them from the Vestry. The Vestry was the entire parish which was charged to take care of the parish property. The "select Vestry" was a group of leading men elected by the parish to care for the parish poor. During the early 1600s, additional duties were added to those of the Vestry in Virginia, including maintenance of the roads and ferry service over the rivers. The church was, in fact, the governmental agency for colonial Virginia. It maintained all of the records of births, marriages, and deaths.

About this time, the original borough church for the Elizabeth River Parish was established on Mr. Sewell's land which was located roughly at what is now Gate 2 of Naval Station Norfolk. On May 25, 1640, a Mr. Harrison was employed as the minister for a "parrishe church at Mr. Sewell's Point" as reflected in a court order. In 1641, the church moved to the end of Crab Creek near where

Hughart and Little Creek roads intersect today. Neither of these wooden buildings remain. Since everybody was required by law to attend church on Sundays, the church established "Chapels of Ease" throughout the area. One was located near the spot of the current St. Paul's in Norfolk, another in Portsmouth and a third in Chesapeake, then called St. Bride's.

In 1662-1663, the General Assembly established the number to serve on a Vestry to be twelve. One of the most important duties of the Vestry was setting the annual parish levy, which was usually the largest tax paid by the colonists. The parish levy provided for the minister's salary and for the poor of the parish. Generally, 25% to 30% of the parish budget would be spent on the poor. Additional duties of the Vestry included serving as "tobacco viewers" to ensure that there wasn't too much tobacco being planted, to serve as church wardens who presented moral offenders to the county courts, and "going round... the bounds of every person's land" every four years to reset the property boundary markers.

The future of Norfolk as a seaport began to take shape when in 1670 a royal decree demanded the establishment of warehouses in each of the then-existing twenty counties. In 1736, the Borough of Norfolk was established by Royal Decree. On April 1, 1754, Robert Dinwiddie, the Royal Lieutenant Governor of Virginia, presented a silver ceremonial Mace to the Norfolk Common Council as a symbol of authority. Historically, maces were weapons made of heavy metal to protect the nobility. The Norfolk Mace is a cherished part of Norfolk's history and is on display at the Chrysler Museum of Art.

Christ & St. Luke's Church has five pieces of Colonial Silver which are also a part of the heritage of Norfolk. They were given by leading citizens of the town who contributed not only to the Church but also to the city. In 1700, the

The colonial silver in 2016. Photo courtesy of Kevin Kwan

Elizabeth River Parish church received a silver chalice as a gift from Captain Samuel Boush, Norfolk's first mayor when the town was incorporated in 1736. Colonel Robert Tucker, the owner of a brigantine as well as three keel (flat-bottomed) boats and three sloops, all used for trade with Bermuda, a frequent trading partner of the Virginia colony, gave a silver chalice and paten to the parish in 1722. As memorial gifts, Captain Whitwell donated an alms basin in 1749 and Christopher Perkins donated a flagon in 1762.

As NORFOLK GREW into the primary town in the area, the Elizabeth River Parish was built on the site of a former "chapel of ease" in 1739. Located at the corner of City Hall Avenue and "The Road that Leadeth Out of Town," it was built of Flemish brick in the sign of the cross. Samuel Boush contributed the bricks for the building. In later years, this would become Norfolk's second parish, St. Paul's.

The General Assembly dissolved the original Elizabeth

River Parish in 1761, declaring that the Vestry was "guilty of some illegal practices, oppressive to the inhabitants thereof." Underlying the strife was the growth in the area. In its place, the General Assembly established three parishes— Elizabeth River Parish, Portsmouth Parish, and St. Bride's Parish. The town of Portsmouth was laid out in 1750 by William Crawford. Portsmouth Parish, now Trinity Church, was erected in 1762. St. Bride's Parish contained all of the land lying between the eastern and southern branches of the Elizabeth River west to the Dismal Swamp and south to the North Carolina state line. A parish church was built on what is now Battlefield Boulevard near its intersection of St. Bride's Road.

Tensions were growing in Norfolk about the same time as the American Revolution began at Lexington and Concord in 1775. In Virginia, those in favor of separating from England controlled the colonial legislature. The Whigs (fondly referred to as the Patriots) began recruiting troops in March, 1775, leading to a struggle with the colonial government, led by Governor Lord Dunmore, for control of military supplies.

When Lord Dunmore's troops took the gunpowder from storage at Williamsburg, tensions increased even further, causing Lord Dunmore to fear for his life. He and his family took refuge on a ship which traveled down the river from Williamsburg to Norfolk. Meanwhile, Lord Dunmore and his forces tried to quell the uprising, an action which only caused the Patriots to grow in numbers. The Virginia militia defeated Lord Dunmore's troops at the Battle of Great Bridge in early December, 1775.

Unlike many Virginia towns, Norfolk remained loyal to the King and became a refuge for the British due to its British-shipping-based economy. By mid-December, the Virginia militia had grown to over 1,200 men. Colonel Robert Howe, a Continental commander from North

Carolina, arrived with reinforcements in Norfolk shortly after the defeat of the British at Great Bridge, with the sole purpose of seizing control of Norfolk from the British. Many of the Loyalists in Norfolk fled to British ships anchored in the harbor. Overcrowded, the ships needed provisions which were denied by Colonel Howe.

In order to gain access to needed supplies, in the afternoon of January 1, 1776, the British began shelling Norfolk from the ships anchored in the harbor. One of the cannonballs hit the side of the Elizabeth River Parish church, giving rise to the "Church with the Ball in the Wall" slogan. Landing parties from the ships entered Norfolk looking for provisions and setting fire to structures which either belonged to Whigs or from which snipers were firing.

But greater damage was done to the town by Colonel Howe's forces. Earlier, understanding that Norfolk could not be protected from the British due to its location, he had recommended it be abandoned.

Patriot forces set additional fires throughout the town and raided it for provisions. Aided by a strong wind, the fire burned for several days destroying the majority of the town. In the end, 863 buildings in Norfolk were destroyed, of which only nineteen were due to the British attack. The Elizabeth River Parish church was severely damaged by the fires.

On the day after Virginia declared its independence from England, the Virginia Convention, which governed not only the Commonwealth of Virginia but also the Church of Virginia, mandated that the prayers for the King and for England be removed from the Book of Common Prayer. Many members of the Clergy throughout Virginia took oaths to the new Commonwealth and a number of them eventually bore arms and fought for independence.

With its historical close association with the Church of England, the Church of Virginia saw its numbers wither as many clergy and congregations remained Loyalists. From a high point of 104 parishes in the Church of Virginia, by 1785 there were only forty parishes remaining. One of those was the Elizabeth River Parish.

CHAPTER 2

The Borough Church

AFTER THE REVOLUTIONARY WAR, things were very difficult for residents of the Norfolk area. Things were also very difficult for the Church of Virginia. During colonial times, taxes had supported the church and its mission. Now the church was left without a means of support as well as without a governing body. To compensate for the loss of revenues, the church established a system of selling pews to members and additionally charging rent for the pews. Those pews that were considered to be well-positioned commanded a higher price and rent.

The Church of Virginia, now an entity separate from the government, quickly established itself in May, 1785, but members of the new General Assembly, fearing it could become the state religion, denied it the ability to incorporate. With the formation of Episcopal Church in Virginia in September, 1785, the church also suffered from internal forces. Primary was the composition of the Vestries. They were self-perpetuating of the "old guard." Individuals tend to associate with people they know and trust, and the same was true in the church: when a Vestryman resigned from the role, it was the Vestry who picked his replacement. The result was, for all practical purposes, an "old boys' club." Because the early members of the "select Vestry" in the colonial church were men of wealth and social status, the same was perpetuated in the newly formed Episcopal Church.

THE ELIZABETH RIVER PARISH experienced a rift in the early 1790s. There were two factions in the church: one was led by Reverend James Whitehead, the rector of the church and headmaster of Norfolk Academy; the other was headed by Reverend William Bland, a man favored by the local ship captains. They held separate services in the church—one in the morning and the other in the afternoon. The larger group, which comprised about 90% of the total congregation, was led by Reverend Whitehead.

At the Diocesan convention of 1792, only one of the two factions could be seated. The Diocese gave credentials to the faction led by Reverend Whitehead. In 1798, the Whitehead faction abandoned the building, possibly because it was in very poor shape or perhaps because its Colonial style was no longer in vogue. The group, totaling about 100 families, met across the street in the Norfolk Circuit Courthouse. The smaller faction led by Reverend Bland, totaling about fifteen families, stayed in the church building.

The Whitehead faction built a new church in 1800 for $16,000. The cornerstone was laid on St. John's Day, June 24, 1800, in an elaborate ceremony. Reverend Whitehead preached from the pulpit of the old Elizabeth River Parish. There was not only a religious laying of the cornerstone but also one using a Masonic Rite led by the Norfolk Lodge #1, A.F. & A.M. The brass plate buried with the cornerstone indicates that it was laid in the presence of the Mayor, the Recorder, the Aldermen, and a large number of citizens. After the festivities, the attendees went to the Borough Tavern on Main Street for dinner.

The church, constructed of brick, was at the northeast corner of Church Street (now St. Paul's Boulevard) and City Hall Avenue on property that is now the Juvenile and Domestic Relations Court of the City of Norfolk. The church had the first pipe organ in Norfolk. Seated on the organ bench was James H. Swindells, the first recorded "minister of music" in Norfolk. Swindells organized a concert featuring music by European composers George Frideric Handel, Giovanni Battista Pergolesi and others on May 21, 1818 to be performed before an audience reported to be in excess of 1,000 people. The concert was so successful that a second performance was held with President James Monroe in attendance. While Swindells was the music director for Christ Church, some excerpts, if not complete oratorios, were sung at the new church.

At the new location, for the first time the church called itself Christ Church. That did not mean that they abandoned the Elizabeth River Parish name. The names were interchangeable and clearly meant this church was still led by Reverend Whitehead.

In 1803, Reverend Bland died and the small congregation, without their leader, ceased to exist. Although the building was occasionally used for Sunday School or by a Baptist congregation, it wasn't maintained and continued to deteriorate. Any tenant for the building had to apply to the Vestry of Christ Church, because title and ownership of the old building remained in the name of the Elizabeth River Parish.

ALTHOUGH THE YOUNG COUNTRY had won independence from Great Britain, the relationship between America and England remained tense. Involved in a war with France, Britain sent ships frequently into the waters off the coast of the United States looking for sailors they could impress into the British Royal Navy. Two French navy vessels had been damaged by a hurricane in September, 1806, off the coast of Virginia and the ships were brought to Norfolk for repair. In order to stop the French vessels from re-entering the war after they were repaired, the British posted two vessels at the mouth of the Chesapeake Bay. Four conscripted sailors—three American and one British—on the British ships took a chance to escape the harsh shipboard life. The four men were seen in Portsmouth by their commanding officers who demanded that the sailors be returned to the British Navy. This demand was ignored.

The foursome had enlisted in the United States Navy and were assigned to the *USS Chesapeake* which was leaving port on June 22, 1807. As the *Chesapeake* cleared Cape Henry, she was approached by *HMS Leopard*, whose captain demanded the return of the four deserters. When the *Chesapeake*'s commander refused, the *Leopard* opened fire on the *Chesapeake*, resulting in the deaths of three sailors and injury to eighteen. The four deserters were forcibly removed from the ship. Severely damaged, the *Chesapeake* returned to Portsmouth.

One of the injured sailors, Robert MacDonald, was taken to Norfolk Marine Hospital where he died several days later. Under normal circumstances, MacDonald's death would have gone unnoticed, but this was different. The firing upon a United States Navy vessel had ignited public opinion against Britain, and MacDonald became a symbol of the outrage. His funeral, conducted by Reverend Thomas Davis of Christ Church, was among the largest ever held in Norfolk.

Robert E. Cray, Jr. in his article, *Remembering the USS Chesapeake,* describes the funeral:

A flotilla of boats, their flags at half-mast, accompanied MacDonald's casket from Hospital Point to Merchant Wharf to the sounds of minute guns. An assemblage of civic officials, military figures, and common citizens about 4,000 strong marched through Norfolk streets following MacDonald's remains to Christ's Church, where the Reverend Davis delivered an "appropriate, impressive, and patriotic discourse."

IN 1822, CHRIST CHURCH acquired a two-manual organ with 25 stops built by Thomas Hall of New York City. Hall was born in England and immigrated to America when he was a child. A few years later, he became an apprentice to John Lowe, another British immigrant. His workmanship reflected his British roots. In the colonial days of the church, congregational singing was usually led by instrumentalists.

Between 1 and 2 a.m. on March 10, 1827, a fire broke out in a wooden building owned by a coachmaker, Elkanah Balance, at the corner of Court and Main streets. Fanned by high winds, the fire raced through the lower section of Church Street (now St. Paul's Boulevard). As the fire approached Christ Church, people removed its furnishings and put them in the street. In an effort to save the church, wet blankets were thrown on the cypress shingle roof, but they did not repel the flames and within an hour the church burned to the ground. Walter Herron, a member of the congregation, had his slaves come assist in the fighting of the fire. Meanwhile, flying embers reached Herron's home, which also went up in flames. The citizens of Norfolk stopped the fire by using gunpowder to blow up buildings in the fire's path.

Reverend Enoch M. Lowe, Rector of Christ Church,

had died February 26, 1823 and was interred in a vault in the floor of the middle aisle. After Christ Church burned, Reverend Lowe's remains were removed to the old church and then on for interment at Cedar Grove Cemetery.

After this catastrophic event, Christ Church abandoned the location of their first building. Later, First Presbyterian Church would build on the site of the first Christ Church.

✠ ✠ ✠ ✠ ✠ ✠ ✠ ✠ ✠ ✠ ✠ ✠ ✠ ✠ ✠

CHAPTER 3

The "Old" Christ Church

LEFT WITHOUT A CHURCH BUILDING, the congregation returned for a while to the old Elizabeth River Parish church, but there was no doubt that this was a temporary facility. The building was in very poor shape and the congregation had outgrown its capacity. The congregation chose to build a new church on Freemason Street.

The congregation laid the cornerstone on June 20, 1827. The ceremony was led by Bishop Richard Channing Moore and included Norfolk's mayor, recorder, and aldermen; the building committee and architect; and numerous clergy from the town. Once again, there was a Masonic Rite performed by the Norfolk Lodge #1, A.F. & A.M. joined by a Portsmouth Masonic Lodge. The brass plate from the Christ Church that had burned was taken to the new site. The new church was at Freemason and Brewer streets.

The front of the church on Freemason Street was 65

This cornerstone is found on the right side of the tower entrance and was taken from the 1827 church. Another cornerstone, to be found on the left hand side of the tower door, commemorates the cornerstone laying in 1909.

23

Exterior of Christ Church facing Freemason Street. This church was built in 1827. Image courtesy of Sergeant Memorial Collection, Slover Library

feet long and the depth on Cumberland Street was 96 feet. Designed by Thomas Williamson, then a cashier at the Virginia Bank, it was of a Greek revival style. The building was constructed by Levi Swain, an architect and contractor.

The dedication of the church on November 9, 1828, was led by Bishop Moore. Rector Dr. Henry W. Ducachet's sermon was "Oh Earth, Earth, Earth, hear ye the word of the Lord." As part of the celebration, Haydn's *Creation* was performed in front of a large audience on November 10, 1828. It was the first performance of *Creation* in Norfolk.

A November 12, 1828 *American Beacon* article described the new church:

> There were 88 pews on the main floor and 42 pews in the galleries. The former divided by a center and two side aisles. The galleries are supported by light and handsome pillars, painted in most excellent imitation of bronze; but the altar and pulpit are the greatest attraction to the eye. The rail-work around the altar is very handsome and bronzed in the best style; and the pulpit is the most chaste and elegant piece of work of the kind we have ever seen. There is an inscription from Jeremiah, in large gilt letters on a cerulean ground, 'O Earth, Earth, Earth, hear the word of the Lord'.

Despite the grandness of the church, there was no attempt to heat it. In the cold winter months, members probably brought heated bricks wrapped in baize, a woolen type of cloth. At an October, 1831, congregational meeting, a plan to heat the church was defeated by a vote of 28 ayes, 40 nays. Perhaps it was a cold snap reminding the congregation of the misery of the cold winter ahead that finally resulted in a resolution to heat the church as soon as possible on December 13, 1831.

The church was rarely used at night, due to a lack of lighting which depended upon oil lamps. Its pews with doors which swung to the inside were deep, about 1½ times the depth of Christ & St. Luke's current pews, and had boxes to hold the fashionable tall hats.

A bell and a clock were planned for the 130-foot church spire. The bell was cast in Norfolk by Philadelphia native Stephen Russell at his Briggs Point foundry at a cost of $419.95. There is a story that when the bell was being cast, some members of the congregation visited the foundry and threw in some of their silver, thus endowing the bell with a particularly melodious tone.

Interior of old Christ Church. Photo courtesy of Sergeant Memorial Collection, Slover Library

At a cost of $863.63, the clock was designed and built by Isaiah Lukens of Philadelphia, probably the best known clock maker of his era. Lukens also made the clock which was in Independence Hall in Philadelphia. The clock was brought down to Norfolk aboard the boat *Naomi* arriving on November 28, 1828. After the installation of the clock, it became the town's clock. Interconnected to the bell, a hammer would strike the bell when the clock would reach each passing hour.

One member of the parish, a Commodore Crane, gave the church a large marble flower vase with handles shaped like serpents which he had purchased in Italy. For years after the congregation built the 1828 building, this vase was used as the baptismal font. A bowl for the water was placed inside of the vase. At one baptism, a youngster went fleeing to the back of the church and hid under a pew. The rector followed the youngster, bowl in hand, and baptized the child.

The congregation grew and by 1831 had outgrown the building. With 230 communicants, it was the largest congregation in the Diocese of Virginia. The minutes of the Trustees of Christ Church from July 1, 1831 reflected the need to establish a new congregation. "A communication was handed in by Mr. Steed from the Reverend. Dr. Ducachet on the subject of getting up another Episcopal congregation for the old church."

Under the leadership of Reverend Dr. Ducachet, the congregation repaired the old borough church building which was renamed St. Paul's. The new church was planted on April 24, 1832. The congregation for St. Paul's drew heavily from the congregation of Christ Church. Of the five Vestrymen appointed for St. Paul's, four continued on the rolls of Christ Church. In the early days of St. Paul's, Christ Church provided both the minister as well as financial support.

In 1834, St. Paul's Church was modified to include a square tower over the gable with a window on each side. In each corner of the tower, there were short spires which were surmounted by a gilded Latin Cross. Colonel William Lamb told the following tale, probably heard from his parents:

> Never was there a greater tempest in a teapot than was created by those four innocent crosses. A large portion of the congregation were outraged and some of the influential members of Christ Church, who felt spiritually responsible for St. Paul's as the weaker congregation, were moved beyond measure. Whether the souls of our neighboring Methodist brethren, our Baptist friends, or the sterling covenanters [Scottish Presbyterians] across the way were disturbed in their Sunday worship by the sudden apparition under their

The four spires of St. Paul's Church are visible in this image.
Source: Howe, Henry. Historical Collections of Virginia:
Charleston, S.C.: Babcock & Co, 1845. p. 395.

windows of the quadruple emblem of Rome we do
not remember, but we shall never forget that one good
Catholic, our friend Eli Barrot, was reported to have
some a solemnly protested against the innovation, as
on his way to and from business to his home, as he
passed the old church, he was forced to cross himself
four times.

Quickly, the Vestry ordered that the crosses be removed
from the tower. Instead, Colonel Lamb described the
substitution. "And for want of some unobjectionable
substitute, four gold bowls replaced in their stead, as if some
celestial planets of the smaller sort had fallen from space
and then impaled on the points of the spires." These golden
spheres remained until 1901 when they were replaced by
the current spire.

Henry Erben, an apprentice of Thomas Hall, built a
three-manual organ for Christ Church in 1843. Erben, one

of the leading organ builders in the United States, built an organ for Trinity Church Wall Street in 1846.

One of the great orators of the old Christ Church was Reverend George D. Cummins who was called in 1847. The power of his sermons resulted in the church often being filled to capacity. Even those from other denominations came to hear him preach. One Roman Catholic even purchased a pew in the church for $290. Reverend Cummins' reputation spread quickly throughout the Norfolk community and by December, 1847, it was obvious that additional seating was needed. Forty-seven of the ground floor pew-holders agreed to a plan to alter their pews. By doing this, the church gained an additional eighteen pews.

One warm Sunday, Reverend Cummins' preaching attracted a most unusual visitor: a chicken had wandered in from outside. It came down the aisle, hopped up the steps

Street view of old Christ Church. Photo courtesy of VU Photos, Sargeant Memorial Collection, Slover Library

and perched on the ledge beside Reverend Cummins who kept on preaching the sermon as if this was an everyday occurrence.

Reverend Cummins resigned his position at Christ Church in July 1853 having accepted a call from St. James Church in Richmond. He would lead several other parishes before being consecrated as a bishop in the Diocese of Kentucky. In the early 1870s, there was dissent within the Episcopal Church over excessive ritualism and the exclusive attitude in the Episcopal Church towards other religions. When Bishop Cummins was criticized for participating in a Eucharist at Fifth Avenue Presbyterian Church in New York City, he, along with six other ordained priests and twenty lay parishioners, created the Reformed Episcopal Church. The Right Reverend Cummins served as the first Presiding Bishop of the Reformed Episcopal Church.

Following the yellow fever epidemic of 1855, Christ Church got a new rector, the Reverend Erskine Madison Rodman. Originally from New York, he was educated at Columbia University before attending Virginia Theological Seminary in Alexandria. While in Alexandria, he met his future wife, Anne Selden.

On August 31, 1858, the Christ Church organist, Professor Philip H. Masi, led a group of soloists in the first performance of Rossini's *Stabat Mater* in the recently completed St. Mary's Catholic Church. Professor Masi was the leading musician in Norfolk, and in 1878 composed "Nearer, My God, To Thee" for two soloists and choir.

ALTHOUGH HE WAS originally from the North, during the Union occupation of Norfolk Reverend Rodman liked to argue with Egbert Viele, the Military Governor of Norfolk, and General Benjamin Butler. Reverend

Rodman was also arrested several times for not taking an oath of allegiance to the United States. Having had enough of his combativeness, the Union authorities put Reverend Rodman and his family on a train for New York. He returned to Norfolk by way of Liverpool, England, and Nassau, and finally on a blockade runner. Back in the South, Reverend Rodman served as chaplain to the Confederate forces. After the Civil War, Reverend Rodman returned to the north where he served as Rector of Grace Church in Plainfield, New Jersey, for thirty-two years.

✠

JUST LIKE THE LIBERTY BELL, the bell of Christ Church cracked as it was rung by the church sexton in 1859. A new bell was ordered from Maneely & Sons of West Troy, New York. It arrived in Norfolk on June 5, 1860. The old Russell bell was rung one last time on June 6, 1860 after which it was removed from the church steeple and replaced by the Maneely & Sons bell. The new bell weighed 1,618 pounds.

The Christ Church clock was very important in the daily life of Norfolk residents. Gotlieb Mayer, a timekeeper, was hired by the Select Council of the City of Norfolk on November 16, 1865. Mayer's duties included winding and regulating the clock at a salary of $50 per year. This position continued until 1904.

After the Civil War, Christ Church hired the Reverend O. S. Barten as its rector. Born in Hamburg, Germany, Reverend Barten immigrated to the United States as a young child. He graduated from General Seminary in New York City. Arriving in Norfolk in 1865, he would serve Christ Church as a much beloved rector until his death in 1897.

BY 1880, the Erben organ was showing its age and was in need of renovation. By then, the craft of American organ building was centered in Boston. Christ Church chose the Boston firm Hook & Hastings to refurbish and expand its organ to 35 ranks. After renovating the organ, Hook & Hastings put their nameplate on the organ and called it Opus 1252. The organ was used by Christ Church until the church moved to the Olney Road location in 1910. Today, the Hook & Hastings organ "Opus 1252" continues to be played at the Congregational United Church of Christ in Pawtucket, Rhode Island.

PROBABLY DURING Reverend Barten's tenure, there was a young boy who attended services with his family. Aged probably three or four, his antics must have caused great consternation. In those days, prayers were said on the knees facing away from the chancel with the arms on the seats. One day, while his family was kneeling and praying and thus not watching his every move, he decided that the back of the pew would make a wonderful imaginary horse. He "rode" up and down the back of the pew. Then he spotted a man bent over in prayer whose back looked like it could also be a make-believe horse. Imagine the surprise of the man!

Eventually, to his mother's relief, the child matured and grew less noisome. But that didn't stop his mischievousness. One Sunday he discovered that one of the pew cushions had a small hole in it, and worked quietly but determinedly at enlarging the hole. When it got to a considerable size, he put his head through the hole... and then panicked when he couldn't get the cushion off his head. His muffled

cries resulted in his being extricated from the situation...
and a reaffirmation that he still wasn't behaving.

AFTER MANY YEARS of serving as the Baptismal Font, the
marble vase brought from Italy by Commodore Crane was
showing its age. The handles had been broken and repaired

*Baptismal Font given in memory of Andrew Hill Baxter by his
mother. Photo courtesy of Kevin Kwan*

multiple times. When young congregation member Andrew Hill Baxter died in 1883, his mother, Mrs. Sarah Baxter, donated to the church a new Baptismal Font as a memorial to her son. Made of creamy marble, the Baptismal Font has eight carved sides representing the seven days of Creation and with the final panel portraying the Incarnation. Today it sits in the Selden Chapel near the door. Its placement symbolizes the entry of

This small brass cross was given by the children of Christ Church in memory of their friend, Andrew Hill Baxter. Photo courtesy of Kevin Kwan

The brass eagle lectern was given by the Ladies Guild in memory of Alexina Taylor Page. Photo courtesy of Kevin Kwan

the Baptized into the Christian life.

Additionally, the Sunday School children gave a small brass cross for use in the Sunday School as a memorial to their lost friend, Andrew Hill Baxter.

Also given in 1883 was the brass eagle lectern by the Ladies Guild in memory of Alexina Taylor Page.

Artist's sketch of Christ Church. The sketch includes a Rectory between the church and Pelham Place. Sketch courtesy of Sargeant Memorial Collection, Slover Library

DR. JOHN JACOB MILLER became the organist and choir director of Christ Church in December 1889. Born near Jefferson City, Missouri, he held several church positions as a youngster. After studying at the Hershey School of Music under Clarence Eddy, he became the organist at St. John, Quincy, Illinois. In 1885, he became the organist/choirmaster at Grace Church in Middletown, New York where he started a boys' choir. He also was the supervisor of music for the public schools in Middletown, New York.

Over his thirty-nine year career in Norfolk, Miller was instrumental in bringing many famous musical artists and orchestras to Norfolk. Under his leadership, the Norfolk area was treated to its first performances of Handel's *Messiah*, Mendelssohn's *Elijah*, and Bach's *Passion According to St. Matthew*. Miller also served as the organist of Ohef Sholom Temple. It was in 1909, during his tenure at Christ Church, that the church instituted a choir of men and boys in preparation for the move to Olney Road.

Talk of relocating Christ Church from downtown began in the early 1900s just as the new suburb of Ghent was being built. The church purchased four lots at the intersection of Olney Road and Stockley Gardens for a total cost of $8,500 with the hope of someday building a handsome edifice. With more Episcopalians residing in Ghent, members of the three downtown churches (St. Paul's, Christ Church and St. Luke's) banded together to build a simple wooden chapel on the site for $3,000. St. Stephen's Chapel had a seating capacity of 200 and had a Flemish oak finish. It was, effectively, a "chapel of ease" for the Ghent residents who could attend Sunday night and mid-week evening services at the Chapel.

Discussions were ongoing by members of the Christ Church congregation about the possibility of relocating to Ghent. Not everyone was in favor of the move, particularly those who lived in the downtown area. At a December 1906 parish meeting, 125 members wanted to continue to worship at the old Christ Church. They were in a minority and soon the congregation would begin making plans for a new building.

CHAPTER 4

Building of a New Church

IN JUNE 1908, Christ Church hired the Reverend Francis W. Steinmetz as rector. Reverend Steinmetz had served as an assistant at the historic Christ Church in Philadelphia before becoming the rector of Christ Church, Ridley Park in 1898. During his tenure at Ridley Park, Reverend Steinmetz brought in many distinguished university professors to preach at the church. He also instituted the envelope system for payment of pledges.

Reverend Steinmetz, who was actively involved in the building of Norfolk's Christ Church structure, got his feet wet during his tenure at Christ Church, Ridley Park. In 1901, that church went through an expansion phase which included the enlargement of the chancel and the addition of transepts and cross aisle as well as significant modifications to the church. On the fifteenth anniversary of his call to Norfolk, he said one of the attractions of the position of rector was the opportunity to build a new church.

With strong ties to the Philadelphia area, Reverend Steinmetz selected the firm of Watson & Huckel for the architectural design. Both Frank R. Watson and Samuel Huckel, Jr. were from the Philadelphia area.

AFTER GRADUATING from high school, Watson joined the firm of Edwin F. Durang who had a reputation for designing Roman Catholic churches during the 1880s and 1890s. After five years with Durang, Watson established his own firm with a branch office in Atlantic City, New Jersey, which completed a wide variety of projects ranging from churches to commercial buildings, apartments, and houses.

Huckel studied painting before joining the office of Benjamin D. Price, who specialized in church architecture and window painting. Watson & Huckel joined forces in 1901 and designed many churches and other commercial buildings primarily in the Philadelphia area including the Church of the Epiphany (Catholic). Among the designs were the Union Station in Worcester, Massachusetts, the Courthouse in Bridgeton, New Jersey, and the Monmouth Hotel in Spring Lake, New Jersey.

While Watson & Huckle were selected as the architects for the new Christ Church building, it was also necessary to have local architects to manage the construction of the structure. The firm of Ferguson, Carlow & Taylor was selected. The church selected E. Tatterson as the general

St. Stephen's Chapel, in 1909. In front of the chapel, Christ Church is beginning to rise. Courtesy of Christ & St. Luke's archives

39

contractor. He was based in Norfolk and had built, among others, the Virginia Club building located at the corner of Granby and Plume streets in 1903-1904.

St. Stephen's Chapel was originally located on the lot adjacent to the Pelham apartments fronting Olney Road. During the construction process, St. Stephen's Chapel continued to hold Morning Prayer and Evening Prayer. The primary Sunday services for the congregation during construction continued to be held at the old Christ Church building.

THE CORNERSTONE for Christ Church in the new suburb of Ghent was laid on Saints Simon & Jude Day, October 28, 1909. In accordance with tradition, on one of the entrances to the church was a new cornerstone. On the other side of the entrance is the old cornerstone from the Christ Church buildings of 1800 and 1827. As with the two earlier Christ Church buildings, there were both religious and Masonic ceremonies at the laying of the two cornerstones. The religious ceremonies were led by the Right Reverend Alfred M. Randolph, Bishop of the Diocese of Southern Virginia, and his assistant, the Right Reverend Beverley D. Tucker. The Masonic rite was done by the Grand Master of Masons of Virginia Joseph W. Eggleston, from the Norfolk Lodge #1.

One of the legends of the cornerstone laying was that President William Howard Taft was present. Although this makes for a great tale, the reality is that President Taft was on a junket floating down the Mississippi River somewhere between Helena, Arkansas and Vicksburg, Mississippi on that October afternoon. Eventually Taft visited Norfolk on November 19, 1909, where he was greeted by a twenty-one-gun salute. He enjoyed a dinner with twenty other guests

The laying of the cornerstone for Christ Church on October 28, 1909. St. Stephen's Chapel is in the background with Pelham Place behind the Chapel. Photo courtesy of Library of Virginia, Mann Collection

including industrialist Andrew Carnegie and Virginia Governor Claude A. Swanson at the home of Fergus Reid, a successful Norfolk businessman and parishioner of Christ Church.

After the laying of the cornerstone, the church building rose. Supported by 1200 pilings 70 feet in length, the nave is 150 feet long and 55 feet in height. The walls are Port Deposit Granite quarried in Maryland. The exterior trimmings for the church are Indiana limestone.

Although the original plans included the tower, the initial construction phase was expected to include building it only to the apex of the church because of the cost. The tower was the most expensive part of the project. The estimated cost of building the church without the tower was

Christ Church is pictured from Mowbray Arch in 1910. Note that the statues of St. Paul and St. Peter are not flanking the front door. To the right in the picture is Pelham Place.

$103,000. As the church rose, so did the tower, regardless of the cost.

During the building of the church, the contractor, E. Tatterson, became ill and subsequently died. Reverend Steinmetz stepped in as the general contractor directing the construction of the church.

The statuary and altars are carved from Caen stone quarried from Normandy, France which gives the altars and statuary the light-creamy yellow color. When Christ Church was built, the traditional placement of the altar was against the chancel wall with the priests facing away from the congregation for the celebration of the Eucharist. Begun during the Middle Ages, this practice had everyone facing toward Jerusalem. As a result of Vatican II in the mid-1960s, a trend swept the world where altars became freestanding. The freestanding altar at Christ & St. Luke's

The interior of Christ Church in 1910. Courtesy VU Photos, Sargeant Memorial Collection, Slover Library

was designed and built in the mid-1970s by parishioner Alex Grice. The detail and painting of it matches the rest of the chancel so that it blends in with the original design.

With the move to Olney Road, the church once again selected the leading organ builder in the country, Austin Organ Company of Hartford, Connecticut. The principal of Austin Organ Company, John Austin, initially learned the craft from his amateur organ-builder father. Austin immigrated to the United States at age twenty. While working for Farrant & Votey Organ Company of Detroit, Austin developed an innovation called the Universal Air Chest. He later went to work at the Clough & Warren Organ Company, also located in Detroit. When that company suffered a devastating fire in 1898, Austin and his brother, Basil, founded the Austin Organ Company. The company continues in business today as Austin Organ, Inc. The organ installed at Christ Church, Opus 278, had 4 manuals with 50 stops.

Historically, Christ Church had a mixed choir of men and women. Dr. Steinmetz' vision for the church was patterned after English cathedrals with a men and boys choir. In 1908, Dr. Miller, the organist and choir director, started the men and boys choir with thirty-five boys and seventeen men. The men and boys choir would be in existence until the 1970s.

BEGINNING IN 1914, the choir of men and boys would sing a Christmas Eve program at the Monticello Hotel in downtown Norfolk starting at 9:30 p.m. By 1925, the carol service had moved into the church and featured traditional carols from the sixteenth century. The primary service in celebration of Christmas was at 11 a.m. on Christmas Day.

In 1915, members of the congregation donated their gold and jewels which were refashioned into a gold

Dr. John J. Miller at the organ console at Christ Church on Olney Road. Photo courtesy of the Library of Virginia, from the Mann Collection

communion set consisting of a chalice and paten. This most probably was suggested by Dr. Steinmetz. Under his tenure, the congregation of Christ Church, Ridley Park, had donated their personal jewelry which was melted down and made into a communion set first used at the services on Easter in 1901.

When the congregation moved to Olney Road, they continued to use the old parish house downtown. It was hoped that funds would soon be available for a new parish house and in 1915, Reverend Steinmetz began a capital campaign. The new parish house would cost between $25,000 and $30,000. The first $1,000 for a new parish house adjacent to the church was raised by the ladies of the church, at which point Reverend Steinmetz challenged the men of the congregation.

The congregation hoped the clock could be moved from the old Christ Church and put into the tower of the new church. Unfortunately, they discovered was that its placement in the tower would render it useless. When the old Christ Church was sold to the Greek Orthodox congregation, the sale exempted the clock which was donated to the College of William & Mary in 1919.

The devastating fire of 1915

In the early morning hours of November 3, 1915, a fire began in the undercroft (basement) of the church. Located directly under the chancel, it quickly spread up through the wind chamber of the organ and reached the roof of the church. At first the only noticeable part of the fire was the smell of smoke but soon people started seeing flames.

The Norfolk Fire Department was unable to do much to put the fire out as their equipment did not reach high enough. Without water reaching the roof of the church, it was soon ablaze. Timbers began falling into the church setting the pews on fire as well as the ornate choir stalls, the rood beam, and the altar rail.

When the fire was finally out, the devastation became clear. The church was open to the elements, the roof having been totally destroyed. The beautiful East Window was estimated at a 90% loss. The West Window (the *Te Deum* window) was considered to be a 50% loss. The clerestory windows were considered a total loss. Six of the statues in the Newton Memorial reredos were cracked including the central figure of Christ as well as the reproduction of

The roof collapse opened the church to the elements. Source: **Christ Church Chronicle,** *Volume 4, Issue 2, November 1, 1915.*

DaVinci's Last Supper. The chancel organ was destroyed and the organ in the tower was heavily damaged by heat. Amazingly, the Selden Chapel suffered little damage.

As men were sweeping the water and timbers out of the church, Reverend Steinmetz was busy on the phone contacting the Austin Organ Company, Mayer & Company (stained glass windows), the stonemasons, and other trades-people who had been involved in the building of the church. All expressed an interest in rebuilding the church. At a Vestry meeting that night, a decision was made to rebuild the church as it was before the fire. The loss was estimated at $50,000 of which $40,000 would be paid by insurance proceeds.

After the Vestry meeting, Reverend Steinmetz traveled to Bedford, Indiana to order more Indiana limestone. It was cut and delivered within two weeks. The roof was replaced by November 20 and the heating system was rebuilt within three weeks. By the end of November, Selden Chapel could be used for services. During the time the church was not available, weekly services were held at a local movie theater, Olef Sholom Temple, and various nearby churches.

Replication of "The Last Supper" part of the Newton Memorial reredos was more difficult. On the day the church burned, there was not a stone in the country large enough to be cut for the tablet. Within two days of the fire, a ship arrived from Caen, France with two stones of adequate size. Both stones had been sold, but one of the buyers was willing to sell the church his stone. The tablet was cut from a stone weighing 11 tons and is 10 feet long. Sculptor J. A. Brickhouse of Philadelphia cut the tablet in the Lychgate Garden in February 1916.

After the devastating fire of 1915, Christ Church once again hired Austin Organ Company to build a new organ. Opus 619 had 4 manuals with 40 stops producing a warm sound reminiscent of an orchestra. The organs of this era produced a sound similar to those of English Cathedrals. This organ served Christ Church for over 50 years.

The commitment of those involved in the rebuilding of the church was evidenced by the reopening of the church a mere five months later on Easter Sunday, April 21, 1916.

The total cost of the rebuilding of the church had increased to $60,000, of which $40,000 was from insurance proceeds.

The building of the Parish House

In 1918, the church received a $25,000 donation from John H. Rogers to build a parish house. Frank R. Watson, the architect of the church, drew the plans for a three-story parish house constructed of rough granite with Indiana limestone trimmings designed to meld in with the existing

The Parish House built in 1918. Picture courtesy of Kevin Kwan

church. Having suffered the effects of the 1915 fire, the "fire proof" building would be made entirely of concrete. The English basement consisted of two club rooms—one for men and the other for boys. Each would have a fireplace, a billiard table and a small gymnasium. The first floor would contain two sacristies, a guild room, a large choir room and a public "retiring" room. The second floor was designed to have a large auditorium with a seating capacity of 500 with a stage, a kitchen, and rooms to be used for Sunday School. The estimated cost of construction was $35,000.

Patriotic fever was high when the United States entered World War I. Serving in the Armed Forces during the conflict were 112 parishioners. Reverend and Mrs. Steinmetz had particular interest in one member of the U.S. Navy—their son, Karl, who enlisted in April 1918. Karl was aboard the *USS San Diego* when it left Portsmouth, New Hampshire escorting some vessels to New York. It was either hit by a torpedo or it hit a mine about 13½ miles off Fire Island, New York. The ship sank in twenty-eight minutes. Amazingly, only six of the crew of 1,183 died. Karl was among those who survived.

In 1922, the Vestry adopted a plan to erect statues on the columns in the nave and choir. The statues are a little over four feet high. The first two statues subscribed are the ones to St. Simeon in the memory of Nathaniel Beamon and the other, Anna, is in memory of Mrs. Katherine Campbell Groner.

ON REVEREND STEINMETZ' fifteenth anniversary at Christ Church Norfolk, the church was consecrated by the Right Reverend Beverley D. Tucker as the debt had been paid off. In a mere twelve years, the parish had paid off not only the original debt on the church but had also the debt incurred because of the fire and the cost of building

When the statues were carved, a full sized model would first be made to ensure that it would fit within its niche. This is a photo of the mock-up of the Louis Pasteur statue.

the parish house. The music for the day included Mozart's *Mass in B flat*.

For several years, Christ Church maintained a cottage at Willoughby Spit. While some of the youth were there on July 4, 1922, a fire broke out in an adjacent cottage. Without a fire department in close proximity to the building, the boys went into the burning structure and removed the mattresses and bedding. They then began to fight the fire which saved the cottage from destruction.

Two years later, the Christ Church cottage at Ocean View was destroyed. In November 1925, a parishioner of the church offered property at the oceanfront near Dam Neck Mills and near the lifesaving station. It had a small two-story house which was furnished with bunks and mattresses.

⊗

ONE AMUSING STORY of the church recounts an Easter Sunday during Professor Miller's tenure as organist/choirmaster. George Tucker, who was a chorister under Professor Miller, told the following tale.

> One of the acolytes that morning was a small boy whose mother had talked the reluctant rector into allowing her son to serve on the altar. Tricked out in white and scarlet, the pint-sized functionary went through his paces perfectly until it came time to take up the offering. It was a feast day and the collection was proportionately large. And as the usher piled the overflowing silver plates into the huge alms basin he held out unsteadily, it dawned on every choirboy looking on apprehensively that he would never make it to the high altar. A flourish of trumpets diverted us momentarily, and we swung toward the altar to sing the Doxology. The overburdened acolyte also pivoted at the same time. Suddenly there was a crash of silver alms basins. Cash and church envelopes flew in all directions. But the miniscule acolyte doggedly bore what was left to the altar. Since there was no possible way the spilled cash could be retrieved until after the service, we could hardly sing for looking at the tempting loot flung so advantageously in our path. When the recessional finally got under way, it was a case of "Let not thy right hand know what the left is doing." Balancing his hymnal on one hand, each choir boy did a little private retrieving as he passed out

The Selden Chapel with the Angel of the Annunciation (Angel Gabriel) in the early 1920s. Photo courtesy of the Library of Virginia, Mann Collection

of the chancel. The ill-gotten gains were soon back where they belonged. Having taken in the situation from his organ bench, Professor Miller locked us in the practice room, secured the assistance of a hefty tenor, and shook us down to the tune of more than $100 before we were permitted to go home and eat our Easter Sunday dinner.

World War I Soldiers and Sailors Tablet dedicated

On May 31, 1925, the stone tablet dedicated to the soldiers and sailors serving the county during World War I was dedicated as part of an evensong. The service opened with a procession which included the choir, followed by armed guard soldiers and the procession of the flags of the United States, Virginia, and the Norfolk Mace thus representing the country, the state, and the city.

Inscribed upon the top of the twelve-foot-square tablet is "This tablet is erected by St. Mary's Guild of Intercession to honor the loyal men and women of this congregation who served their country in the great World War 1917–1918." Following that are the names of the 112 parishioners who served during World War I. Although two were seriously injured, there were no casualties from Christ Church.

St. Mary's Guild of Intercession was created to send letters and packages to servicemen when the United States entered World War I. The lintel of the tablet is inscribed with the seals of the City of Norfolk, the Commonwealth of Virginia, and the arms of the Allied Nations (England, France, Belgium, and Italy). This is surmounted by the shield and eagle of the United States and flags from the Allied countries. At the very top of the tablet is a cross. On the sides of the tablet are two niches containing statues. The one on the left side is of a knight in armor, representing war, while the one on the right is a woman holding music, representing peace. The face of the knight is Reverend Steinmetz while the face of the woman is Mary Steinmetz, Reverend Steinmetz's wife.

The service included patriotic music and the organ was supplemented by a brass ensemble and timpani. The unveiling of the tablet was at the very end of the service that included a homily by Reverend Steinmetz.

Purchase of the Guild House

The Guild House which stood for years at the corner of Stockley Gardens and Boissevain Avenue was purchased as a Rectory for the church for $35,000. Originally it had twenty rooms, including ten bedchambers.

The departure of Reverend Steinmetz

In keeping with traditional English Cathedral architecture, the church building contains a chapel. Dedicated to the memory of the Selden family, it is located on the west side of the main nave. Like the high altar, the chapel was designed to have a reredos. The first statue in the Selden Memorial Chapel reredos was of the Angel of the Annunciation (the Angel Gabriel). The remainder of the reredos niches remained empty.

The interior of Selden Chapel in 1910. The statue of the Angel Gabriel stands in the center reredos.

IN 1925, THE VESTRY approved five additional memorials in the Selden Chapel. The memorials included a stone lectern dedicated to the memory of Mary Selden Grandy Gillmor who died in 1917 leaving two small children; two altar wings in memory of Mary Selden Grandy Gillmor's parents, Wiley Cyrus Grandy (1839-1919) and Mary Selden Grandy (1843-1918); and two stone clergy stalls, one of which is in memory of Mabel Dickman Grandy, the wife of Charles R. Grandy. The stone lectern was soon to become a center of controversy.

Unbeknown to Vestry and the Selden/Grandy family, Reverend Steinmetz replaced the statue of the Angel of Annunciation with a statue of the Virgin Mary. He planned to utilize the statue of the Angel Gabriel in the stone lectern. The substitution was discovered one day by Charles R. Grandy, part of the Selden family. Mr. Grandy immediately protested to Reverend Steinmetz. After gaining no satisfaction from Reverend Steinmetz, Mr. Grandy drew this substitution to the attention of the Vestry who directed Reverend Steinmetz to return the Angel Gabriel to its rightful place. Reverend Steinmetz adamantly refused. Mr. Grandy's objection to the statue of the Virgin Mary shouldn't have been a surprise to Reverend Steinmetz. As early as 1919, Mr. Grandy had written to the architect, Mr. Watson, about the Selden Chapel saying "… changing the reredos as shown on your plan for the end wall of the chapel, except that we all want the center figure retained, and do not want the figure of the Virgin put in the chapel."

On November 8, 1926, the Vestry in an 8-to-1 vote adopted a resolution directing the church wardens, John N. Sebrell and George H. Lewis, and a member of the Vestry, Minton W. Talbot, to restore the statue of the Angel

Gabriel to its place in the reredos, and allocating $300 for this purpose. In response, an injunction was filed in the Norfolk Circuit Court by State Senator James S. Barron on behalf of Reverend Steinmetz to prevent the Wardens from replacing the statue of the Virgin Mary.

Reverend Steinmetz maintained that when he was installed as the rector of the church he was given keys to the church. He interpreted this to mean that he was vested with the authority and control over the church and its properties. He maintained that the trustees, Vestrymen or church wardens didn't have any lawful right and power to deprive him of the powers vested in him by the laws of the Church and State.

Photo by Charles S. Borjes of Christ Church from the Hague in the 1930s. Courtesy of the Sargeant Memorial Collection, Borjes Collection, Slover Library

In the response to the injunction, the Vestry maintained that the Selden Chapel was given with the express provisions in writing that no memorial should be installed in the chapel without the consent in writing of the donors and the Vestry. It went on to further state that Reverend Steinmetz had approached the donors on several occasions for their consent of the replacement of the Angel of Annunciation statue with that of the Virgin Mary, and those requests had been consistently denied.

The Vestry also maintained that under the church canons, the rector controls the worship but everything relating to church property was vested in the authority of the Vestry. They pointed to the general canons which said "the Vestry shall be the agents and legal representatives of the parish in all matters concerning its corporate property and the relations of the parish to the clergy." Steinmetz argued that the Vestry had agreed to the replacement of the Angel of Annunciation in the reredos upon the ordering of the five new memorials.

On January 29, 1926, the court rendered its decision. Judge A. R. Hankle ruled that the temporal and material affairs of an Episcopal church were vested in the Vestry and the authority of the rector ends with the control of the spiritual affairs of the church. The following day, Reverend Steinmetz announced his departure from Christ Church effective at the end of the month. He returned to Philadelphia. The statue of the Virgin Mary was taken to the Norfolk Museum of Arts (now The Chrysler Museum) for safekeeping.

Dean Peacock becomes Rector of Christ Church

With the departure of Reverend Steinmetz in 1927, Christ Church called the Dean of the Cathedral of Mexico City, Howard Dodson Peacock. Dean Peacock was born in England in 1880. During World War I he fought with

Canadian troops. Afterwards, he was called to be the Dean of the Cathedral of Mexico City. While in Mexico City, Dean Peacock grew to know the Morrow family. Dwight Morrow, Sr. was the ambassador to Mexico, and his daughter, Anne, would marry the 1927 aviation hero Charles Lindbergh.

Dean H. Dodson Peacock, rector of Christ Church from 1927 to 1935, instituted several traditions that carry down to today. In 1929, on Palm Sunday, he started the Procession of the Palms, believed to be the first in Virginia. The procession the first year was fairly simple but by 1933, the procession included a crucifer with a veiled cross followed by an acolyte with a cluster of palms and torchbearers. Departing from the normal procession, Dean Peacock inserted several trumpeters before the choir. Following a second crucifer and torchbearers was Dean Peacock.

One of the longstanding relationships of Christ & St. Luke's Church is with The Williams School. In 1930, the school began its tradition of singing carols. The children, dressed in red and green costumes of old English carolers, sang the first year at the Hague beginning at 5 p.m. on a December day. On one December day, the weather was inclement. Not wanting to see the children out in the cold, Dean Peacock invited them into the church. The tradition continues to this day with the children, led by the 8th grade, marching from the school to the church. Many graduates and parents attend the carol service at the church in mid-December.

After the church's longtime organist, Dr. John J. Miller retired in 1928, Christ Church hired George Maxon Vail as the organist and choirmaster in January 1928. Vail grew up on Long Island, New York. A graduate of the Guilmant Organ School in New York, Vail held a number of church positions in New York City. Vail relocated to Norfolk in 1921 to be the organist/choirmaster at St. Paul's. He also

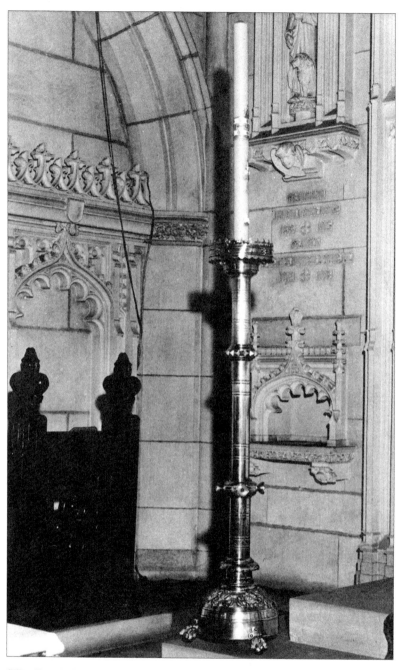

The Paschal Candle was made from a gas candelabra from the old Christ Church.

was a music editor for H. W. Gray music publishing firm and composed a number of church anthems including *King All Glorious* which is still in print and occasionally performed.

Dean Peacock also introduced the Paschal Candle to the church. One of the early symbols of the church, the Paschal Candle represents our Lord's presence with his disciples during the forty days after his resurrection. In 1932, Dean Peacock borrowed a Paschal Candle and began this tradition at Christ Church. Unable to borrow a suitable candle in a subsequent year, he had a gas candelabra from the old Christ Church converted into a stand for the Paschal Candle. The gas candelabra was given by Miss Minnie Leigh Tunis in 1883. An inscription on the base of the Pascal Candle says "The true light which lighteth every man that cometh into the world." Made of brass, it stands about 5 feet tall and the candle, which is about 5 inches wide is also 5 feet in length. The Paschal Candle is lit at the celebration of Easter and remains lighted for all services during the fifty days of Easter. Today, the Paschal Candle is also lighted at baptisms to represent the light of Christ.

❋ ❋ ❋ ❋ ❋ ❋ ❋ ❋ ❋ ❋ ❋ ❋ ❋ ❋ ❋

CHAPTER 5

The Lindbergh Kidnapping

MAN FIRST TOOK FLIGHT in 1903 when the Wright brothers flew the first powered airplane at Kitty Hawk, North Carolina. Automobiles were in their ascendancy and powered flight soon became another challenge. At first, airplanes were a novelty. Barnstormers crossed the country taking passengers up in the air for short flights. In World War I, military battles extended to the air. Captain Eddie Rickenbacker gained fame as an "ace" with twenty-seven aerial victories over Axis powers.

In 1919, Raymond Orteig, an immigrant to the United States, offered a $25,000 prize for the first person to cross the Atlantic in a nonstop flight. Many people dreamed of winning the Orteig prize—it was a great deal of money. One of the people dreaming of winning the prize was an unknown aviator, Charles Lindbergh. On May 20, 1927, Lindbergh in his *Spirit of St. Louis* plane lifted off from Roosevelt Field on Long Island, New York. He landed in Paris, France thirty-three hours later.

Immediately, he was an international hero and was feted from coast to coast. Eventually he would marry Anne Morrow. In 1930, they had a son, Charles Lindbergh, Jr. On the evening of March 1, 1932, the twenty-month-old toddler was kidnapped from the family's home in New Jersey. Across the nation, newspapers told the news of the kidnapping. This quickly became the crime of the century and the nation was focused on every twist and turn in the search for the child.

The kidnapping of the child took a local twist. On the evening of March 9, John Hughes Curtis, a local boat builder, was approached by a bootlegger in the parking lot of a local marina. The bootlegger solicited Curtis to be an intermediary between the kidnappers and Lindbergh. Curtis responded that he didn't want to be involved. He couldn't sleep that night and the next day he decided to consult with Christ Church Rector Dean Peacock. According to *Their Fifteen Minutes: Biographical Sketches of the Lindbergh Case*, Curtis recalled, "Early in the morning I called Dean Dobson-Peacock and asked him to come over and see me... he came over...and I went into detail. We decided that the only to do was to try to get in touch with Lindbergh."

Dean Peacock and Curtis tried to call Lindbergh but Lindbergh's private secretary wouldn't put the call through. They then decided to write Lindbergh but still received no response.

Curtis' wife suggested they enlist the help of Rear Admiral Guy H. Burrage. After the end of World War I, Burrage had become the Norfolk Naval Yard superintendent where he met the Curtis family. By 1927, the summer during which Lindbergh crossed the Atlantic Ocean in his famous flight, Burrage was the Commandant of Naval Forces in Europe. Lindbergh's return trip to the United States was aboard the *USS Memphis* with Admiral Burrage as his escort. Subsequently, Burrage assumed command of the Fifth Naval District located in Norfolk where, in 1931, he retired from military service. Curtis and Peacock correctly believed Burrage had direct access to Lindbergh.

Burrage agreed to contact Lindbergh by phone. When that failed, Burrage, Peacock and Curtis piled into a car and drove to Hopewell, New Jersey where they met with Lindbergh, and Curtis was able to tell his story. Skeptical about the tale, Lindbergh asked for proof including a photograph of the toddler.

Upon returning to Norfolk, Curtis told Dean Peacock that he received information from the kidnappers that they would return the child for $25,000. Dean Peacock agreed to deliver the message personally to Lindbergh. He took a flight from Norfolk Naval Air Station to the Philadelphia Navy Yard and then traveled by car to the Lindbergh residence. Initially rebuffed at the gate, Dean Peacock wouldn't take no for an answer and his persistence resulted in him meeting with Lindbergh and Colonel H. Norman Schwartzkopf, Superintendent of the New Jersey State Police. Unconvinced that there really was contact with the kidnappers, a statement was issued: "Colonel Lindbergh does not believe the information obtained at Norfolk to be of any specific significance in this case." Yet Curtis, Burrage and Peacock pressed on.

At the midday Easter festival service on March 25 the following prayer was led by Dean Peacock:

> O merciful God, and heavenly Father, Who has taught
> us in The Holy Word that Thou does not willingly
> afflict or grieve the children of men: Look with pity,
> we beseech Thee, upon the sorrows of thy servants, the
> Lindbergh family, for whom our prayers are offered.
> Remember them, O Lord, in mercy; endure their
> souls with patience; comfort them with a sense of Thy
> goodness and give Colonel and Mrs. Lindbergh peace
> through the immediate return of their child. Through
> Jesus Christ, our Lord. Amen.

Meanwhile, the newspaper reported that Curtis had been contacted by someone representing Al Capone who was incarcerated for tax evasion. The Capone representative offered Curtis $150,000 if he would either lead the Capone representative to where the baby was or would turn the baby over. Curtis responded that if his efforts were successful to recover the baby, he would turn the child over to his parents. Curtis later denied that he had been in contact with a Capone representative.

In an effort to have a rendezvous with the kidnappers, they enlisted Charles Consolvo, the owner of the Jefferson Hotel in Richmond, to lend his 85-foot yacht *Macon* for four trips out in the Atlantic. When Lindbergh, Curtis, Dean Peacock, Admiral Burrage, and F. H. Lackman, the yacht's skipper, failed to make contact with the kidnappers, they believed that perhaps it was due to the press coverage. Several subsequent trips were made on other boats, also without success.

To keep the public informed, Dean Peacock and Admiral Burrage held daily press conferences at Norfolk's Monticello Hotel at 11 a.m. Their answers to questions posed by the press were usually "I don't know" or "I can't say." Press reports followed or speculated on the whereabouts of Curtis. There were also reported sightings of Lindbergh's agent in Norfolk.

On April 24, 1932, a story was leaked to the two Norfolk newspapers that the baby would soon return. Dean Peacock is quoted as saying "According to our information, the baby will be returned shortly. We have been in contact with these people (the kidnappers) the last few days." Dean Peacock was so sure of the validity of Curtis' story that he believed the baby would be brought to the Rectory.

By April 27, the Norfolk papers were reporting that the return of the baby was imminent. Burrage was quoted as saying "At this time we can state we have overcome a number of obstacles that have stood between us and our objective," Curtis was believed to have brought the kidnappers and Lindbergh together on or near the Eastern Shore and that negotiations were progressing to where the child's return would occur soon. The New

Jersey State Police added to the optimism with a statement that Lindbergh had been in contact with the kidnappers in Virginia.

The likelihood of the child being returned appeared to increase when local newspapers reported that $25,000 had been deposited in a bank as the good faith ransom money.

On May 6, Lindbergh issued a statement indicating that if the child wasn't returned home by May 9, he would cease negotiations through intermediaries and the New Jersey State Police would become more active in the search.

The baby wasn't brought to the Peacock home. The body was discovered near the Lindberghs' home in a roadside thicket on May 12. Initially the New Jersey State Police relied upon Curtis in the identification and arrest of the ringleaders of the kidnapping gang. Curtis responded by providing the names of his contacts to the police. When this failed to lead to the kidnappers, attention turned to Curtis. At the request of the New Jersey State Police, the Norfolk Police Department took scrapings from the Curtis Chevrolet to determine if it had any New Jersey mud on it. They also opened an investigation as to the whereabouts of Curtis on the day of the kidnapping.

Meanwhile, Curtis, who was being held by the New Jersey State Police, soon admitted under questioning he had concocted the entire hoax. He was arrested and bail was set at $10,000, a very large amount for a misdemeanor. Subsequently, he was found guilty of obstruction of justice and sentenced to one year in jail and a fine of $1,000.

Despite the confession and arrest of Curtis, the case was not closed for the New Jersey State Police. Colonel H. Norman Schwartzkopf also wanted to talk with Dean Peacock and Admiral Burrage about their roles in the hoax. In a meeting at Christ Church, six Norfolk attorneys who were also Vestrymen advised Dean Peacock and Admiral Burrage not to travel to New Jersey to meet with New

Jersey authorities. Following the advice, neither Peacock nor Burrage left Norfolk. The New Jersey State Police ultimately decided that both men had been taken in by Curtis' story and were not involved with the hoax.

CHAPTER 6

St. Luke's Parish

W ANTING TO DO MISSIONARY, educational, and charitable work throughout the city, men parishioners of Christ Church and St. Paul's Church formed a Guild on May 5, 1870 and named it the St. Luke's Guild. Before the end of the year, the Guild wanted to hire a full-time clergyman to do outreach. This request was approved by the Reverend O. S. Barten, Rector of Christ Church, and the Reverend N. A. Okeman, Rector of St. Paul's Church. On December 10, 1870, the Reverend S. C. Roberts was called to fill this position.

From this mission work a new church was born. Both Christ Church and St. Paul's congregations exceeded the buildings' capacity for services in the early 1870s. Eight younger members of the two congregations met to organize a new Episcopal church to be called St. Luke's Episcopal Church.

Beverly Dabney, a lifelong parishioner with roots back to the early days of Christ Church, recalled,

> I later learned how my church came into being: that
> my grandparents had been among the group of younger
> members of old Christ Church (the congregation's
> second building at Freemason and Cumberland streets),
> who, looking to the future decided to form a new
> congregation in a building with free pews erected on
> Granby Street. My grandmother's parents remained

in the old church, built in 1827 to replace the original Christ Church on Church Street (opposite the present St. Paul's Episcopal Church), where my grandmother's grandfather bought pew No. 6 for $300 in 1802. I still have the receipt signed by William Vaughan, mayor, as trustee. In addition to the purchase price, my great-great grandfather had to pay an annual rent of $15.

Initially, services for the new church were held in the chapel of Christ Church and also in the bottom floor of a firehouse station on Talbot Street. On September 23, 1872, a lot was purchased at the corner of Bute and James (now Monticello) streets for $1,400. After funds were raised for the construction of a small church, the cornerstone for the building was laid on April 9, 1873. The church was completed at a cost of $7,400. On January 22, 1874, a resolution was drawn for this new parish as part of the Diocese of Virginia and it was admitted as a new parish by the Diocesan Council on May 22, 1874.

In 1885, Arthur Selden Lloyd, a young Episcopal priest originally from Alexandria, Virginia and educated at Virginia Theological Seminary, was called as the rector of the growing St. Luke's Parish. The church quickly outgrew the facilities, and the small congregation began dreaming of a new church building.

On a blustery Good Friday, March 27, 1891, the Norwegian barque, *Dictator,* was headed for the safety of the Chesapeake Bay. Loaded with Georgia pine, the barque had been damaged earlier in storms and it was heading towards Norfolk for repairs. Gale force winds blew the ship into a sandbar at 37th Street and the Virginia Beach oceanfront. When the mast and rigging fell, the ship's two lifeboats were destroyed. Crowds watching from the Princess Anne Hotel and other beachfront buildings followed the brave attempts by lifesaving crews to rescue the seventeen sailors, and the wife and son of the captain, from the ship that was being torn apart by the rough seas. The Georgia pine, which was part of the cargo of the *Dictator*, washed ashore. When St. Luke's needed wood for its interior, St. Luke's Church bought the salvaged wood.

ON EASTER SUNDAY, 1891, a special collection for a new building raised $31,600. On June 4, 1891, a building committee led by Barton Myers, Sr., a leading citizen and former Norfolk mayor, was designated. Plans for a Romanesque church were drawn by Boston architect W. P. Wentworth and on August 7, 1891, the foundation was laid. The following Easter, a special collection raised an additional $7,000. The next year, with the proceeds of the two special collections plus some borrowed money, an impressive brick structure was built at the corner of Granby

St. Luke's Church at Granby and Bute streets was dedicated on October 18, 1892. Source: Art Work of Norfolk and Vicinity (Virginia). *Chicago: H.W. Kennicott & Co, 1895, p 92*

and Bute streets, where the Federal Courthouse now stands. The building's exterior was of Richmond gray granite and North Carolina brownstone. The cost of the building was $65,000 ($14,000 for land, $40,000 for the building and $11,000 for furnishings). The seating capacity was 1,000 on the main floor with an additional 100 in a gallery. It was connected to the old church building, which eventually became the church's Sunday School. The dedication of St. Luke's Church was held on St. Luke's Day, October 18, 1892.

Reverend Lloyd led St. Luke's Church for fifteen years. In 1900, after paying off all debt on the building, the church was consecrated. Although Reverend Lloyd had recently become the General Secretary for the Board of Missions for the Protestant Episcopal Church, he returned to Norfolk to preach at the consecration of the church building on May 29, 1900.

Between 1901 and 1909, Reverend Lloyd was elected Bishop four times and declined each call. In 1909, he was again called by the church to be a Bishop, and was consecrated as the coadjutor bishop of the Diocese of Virginia. He served in this position for only a year before accepting a call by the Protestant Episcopal Church to be the President of the Board of Missions. In 1921, he was elected the Suffragan Bishop of New York.

St. Luke's was bulging at the seams. With the need for additional space, it established St. Andrew's Chapel at the corner of Graydon and Leigh streets for the members of the congregation who lived in the northern section of Ghent. The opening service was held at St. Andrew's on November 11, 1911 and was led by St. Luke's rector, Reverend David W. Howard.

By 1912, with many Norfolk residents moving to the suburbs (Ghent), the St. Luke's congregation was making plans to build a new church farther north nearer its congregants. There was talk that when the new building

St. Luke's Church on Colonial Avenue. Photo courtesy of Borjes Collection, Sargeant Memorial Collection, Slover Library

was built, St. Andrew's would merge with it. The original St. Luke's building was listed for sale with a value estimated at $150,000.

Beverly Dabney, who grew up at St. Luke's Church, recalled her early childhood spent there. At Sunday School, a collection was taken weekly while the children sang "Hear the pennies dropping, Listen as they fall. Every one for Jesus. He will get them all."

On November 28, 1919, the *Virginian-Pilot* reported that St. Luke's Church had been offered $500,000 for its properties, including the church building and the Sunday School which went from Granby Street to Monticello Avenue. Additionally, the congregation could stay in the current building for a three-year period to allow a new church to be built.

St. Andrew's had grown with a congregation of about 400 members. On July 1, 1920, the cornerstone for a new church was laid with both religious and Masonic ceremonies. St. Andrew's held the first service in the new building, built at a cost of $130,000, on October 9, 1921.

On Monday, May 23, 1921, at about 7:15 in the evening, St. Luke's cupola was struck by lightning during a severe thunderstorm. The switchboard at the Norfolk Fire Department was overloaded with calls coming in and assistance was rendered by the U.S. Navy. The firemen were unable to gain access to the interior of the church as the doors were bolted. By the time they finally gained access by breaking down the doors with axes, the fire had spread to the interior of the church. Despite their best efforts, St. Luke's Church was destroyed in a three-alarm fire.

Years later, parishioner Beverly Dabney recalled the fire:

> I was eight-going-on-nine (as we children counted age, anticipating the next step up to adult status), on a hot evening in late May, when lightning struck St. Luke's Church, and it burned to the ground. That was in 1921. As I remember my reaction, it was a mixture of excitement and inability to grasp the fact that something so absolutely immovable as the church could suddenly cease to exist as I knew it. I could only dimly absorb something of the changed atmosphere in our house. Much later I began to understand my family's feeling of loss.

The pulpit in St. Luke's Church was a memorial to Mary Louise Todd Cooke and it survived the fire. It was given to Old Hungar's Church in Eastville, Virginia. One of the columns in Christ & St. Luke's recognizes this memorial. The Sunday School, untouched by the fire, became the church until St. Luke's built a temporary church at 15th Street and Colonial Avenue.

By 1932, St. Luke's Church had only 432 members in the congregation while its satellite congregation, St. Andrew's in West Ghent, was thriving.

CHAPTER 7

Consolidation of Parishes

B Y THE LATE 1920s, things were already difficult for three churches in Ghent—Christ Church, St. Andrew's and St. Luke's. In February 1929, an article in the *Christ Church Chronicles* proclaimed that Ghent was "over-churched." It went on to rejoice that St. Luke's Church had a potential buyer for its property on Granby Street and that it wouldn't be building on the Colonial Avenue site. To do so, said the article, would be "both suicidal and homicidal." The article also suggested a change to Canonic law prohibiting a church from building within two miles of an existing church.

Christ Church was already having financial troubles before the stock market crash in October 1929 that triggered the Great Depression. The church, which had historically depended upon the sale of pews and pew rents, found those payments consistently behind. The Vestry struggled to balance the books and considered a 10% across the board reduction in salaries. When the former organist and choirmaster, J. J. Miller, was discovered to be "badmouthing" the church, his pension was reduced.

The Great Depression only made the situation worse. Hampton Roads' economy was heavily dependent upon the shipping industry, which was hit hard.

By 1931, St. Luke's Church was in discussions with

the federal government for the sale of the Granby Street property where the old St. Luke's Church building was located. The government wanted to build a new building which would contain a post office, federal courthouse, and offices. On August 16, 1931, the Vestry of St. Luke's Church agreed to sell the property to the federal government for $229,000.

AN APRIL, 1931, article in *Christ Church Chronicles* continued the drumbeat of Ghent being over-churched, and lamented about how quickly the lessons of the past had been forgotten.

> The very thing that actuated the removal of Christ Church from Freemason Street to Ghent, in 1910, was the too-close proximity to one another in "old Norfolk" of the three central churches, yet how soon was that lesson forgot, and the same mistake palpably repeated in the location of the now three central churches in a territory appropriate to one alone. And is there now any one of the three that does not have its financial and other problems as a consequence of this failure to learn from the experience of the past?

Discussions of a merger with St. Luke's Church began in October 1931 when its rector, Reverend Dr. David W. Howard, broached the subject with Dean Peacock. Part of the proposal was that Reverend Howard would be added to the staff of Christ Church but without the demands of parish work, as he was in poor health. Both rectors were amenable to the merger but for the two churches to merge, approval would be needed from both Vestries.

Despite the positive feedback, the Vestry of St. Luke's Church found it difficult to follow through with the next step. Later in October, the St. Luke's Vestry decided to poll the congregation about whether they would like to merge with another church and, if so, which one, or if they would prefer to build a new building. This plan was soon abandoned and the Vestry never sent the questionnaire out to the congregation.

At the November 1931 meeting of the St. Luke's Vestry, approval in principle to merge with Christ Church won by the barest of margins (5–4). One of the hesitations the St. Luke's Vestry had was the pew rental system at Christ Church and they indicated that their willingness to merge, in part, depended upon Christ Church dropping the pew rents.

On November 12, 1931, a meeting of a committee from the two Vestries agreed to the merger, subject to the following parameters:

1) The combined church would be called Christ Church with the understanding that both congregations would share in the assets and properties of the combined churches.
2) Pew rents would be abolished.
3) Reverend Dr. Howard would be on the staff of the new combined church as assistant to Dean Peacock.
4) The existing parochial work of both churches would continue.
5) The Parish House of Christ Church would be expanded to accommodate the activities of both churches.

Still, it was difficult for St. Luke's Church to agree to a merger. There was a movement to talk with St. Andrews as well as Christ Church. Meanwhile, at the November, 1931, St. Luke's Vestry meeting, Reverend Dr. Howard resigned due to poor health.

Rumors were circulating that the committee from St. Luke's had failed to follow through with the agreement that had been reached for the merger. Members of the Christ Church Vestry felt that St. Luke's believed the reason Christ Church was willing to merge was the strong financial position of St. Luke's Church. They had proceeds from the sale of the Granby Street property and a much lower operating cost than did Christ Church, which was seemingly always struggling to balance its budget. The Christ Church Vestry decided to take no further action on a merger unless St. Luke's made an additional overture.

At the December, 1931, St. Luke's Vestry meeting, they decided to have discussions about merging with the Church of the Ascension, which was then located in the Park Place neighborhood at 31st Street and Llewellyn Avenue. They were also busy trying to call a new rector but weren't having much success. They issued two calls which were declined. The Reverend Taylor Willis accepted the church's call on August 30, 1932. Reverend Howard died in December 1932.

After a short time in his position, Reverend Willis called a special meeting of the Vestry of St. Luke's on May 1, 1933 to urge them to build a new building. With no action being taken, he wrote a letter to the Vestry dated January 8, 1934 clearly stating that the church needed to be replaced and the parish house, previously a private residence, was unsuitable. He had two architects draw up plans for a new church with an estimated cost of $120,000 and a parish house with an estimated cost of $40,000. Unfortunately, the proceeds from the sale of the land on Granby Street had been invested and was now valued at $152,000.

On February 14, 1934, Dean Peacock, who was planning to resign effective June 1, 1935, again brought the matter of a merger with St. Luke's Church before the Christ Church Vestry. The proposal was that the two churches would merge at the earliest possible date. Both Dean Peacock and Reverend Willis would be joint rectors of the church with each congregation staying in its existing facility. Effective with the retirement of Dean Peacock on June 1, 1935, St. Luke's Church would move into the Christ Church facility and Reverend Willis would be the rector of the combined church. Dean Peacock would continue to draw his $4,000 annual salary for two years after his resignation from the church.

Christ Church and St. Luke's Church both formed committees to hold joint talks about the proposal. By this time, the Bishop of the Diocese of Southern Virginia, The Right Reverend Arthur C. Thomson was involved. He had witnessed the three Ghent churches' decline in membership and giving during the Great Depression and believed a merger would be beneficial. When the proposal was presented to the St. Luke's Vestry, it resulted in a tie vote (6-6). Bishop Thomson declared that the merger discussions were at an end.

Once again, discussions at St. Luke's turned to building a new church. At the April 1934 Vestry meeting, a building committee was established for the project with a cost not to exceed $125,000 for the building, organ, and furnishings. But there was internal dissent regarding the plan. At the June, 1934, Vestry meeting, a petition of ninety-eight members was presented opposing the building of a new structure. At the meeting, the Vestry also heard people who were opposed to a merger with Christ Church.

Reverend Willis held a congregational meeting on July 1, 1934 presenting the "Rector's Plan," which was to invite other churches to join with St. Luke's Church and if there was a lack of interest, to build immediately. This was approved by a congregational vote. When an inquiry to Christ Church was made, it was discovered that they were now interested in a merger of all of the Ghent Episcopal churches—Christ Church, St. Luke's and St. Andrew's. St. Andrew's wasn't enthusiastic about the proposed merger.

St. Luke's Vestry voted affirmatively for a triple merger in principle, and set a date of September 15, 1934 for decisions to be made.

Because travel in those days was by ship, Dean Peacock and his family were enjoying an extended summer vacation in England. Correspondence was sent to him at his London address about the proposed merger. The plan of the three-way merger had been developed after his departure for England. His expected return to Norfolk wouldn't permit a response by Christ Church by the September 15 deadline established by St. Luke's Church.

When Dean Peacock returned in September, a called meeting of the Vestry was held on September 19, 1934, and approved the establishment of a conference committee to work with St. Luke's and St. Andrew's churches on a potential merger. At the October 10, 1934, Christ Church Vestry meeting, the merger of the three Ghent churches was approved in principle, which included naming Reverend Taylor Willis as rector of the combined church and the Reverend E. Ruffin Jones as minister in charge of St. Andrew's as Article 2 of the resolution.

Bishop Thomson attended a called meeting of the Christ Church Vestry on November 19, 1934 where he read a resolution of the St. Andrew's Vestry which said:

RESOLVED UNANIMOUSLY:

1. That the proposal of Christ Church's Vestry expressed at its meeting of November 17, 1934, for amendments of Article 2 of the draft of contract for the merger of that church with St. Luke's and St. Andrew's, are not satisfactory.

2. That this Vestry disapproves of any further negotiations with Christ Church looking towards any merger, and the existing merger committee of this Vestry is discharged.

18:-CHRIST CHURCH (EPISCOPAL) A REPRODUCTION OF ONE OF ENGLAND'S FAMOUS CHURCHES, NORFOLK, VA.

46189

THE HAGUE AND CHRIST'S EPISCOPAL CHURCH, GHENT BY MOONLIGHT, NORFOLK, VA.

75905

Christ & St. Luke's Episcopal church, one of the historical and architectural landmarks of Norfolk, Virginia, has long been the subject of the postcard trade. These postcards date from the 1930s before the merger of Christ Church with St. Luke's Church.

NK-12—The Haque, showing Christ Episcopal Church, Norfolk, Va.

9A-H1094

CHRIST CHURCH, GHENT, NORFOLK, VA.

The images are reproductions of photographic images that were retouched and hand-colored, and in the case of the nighttime image, heavily so.

Bishop Thomson tried to calm the waters. He believed that there had been a misunderstanding by all and that there had been no intentional or arbitrary attempt to offend any of the clergymen. St. Andrew's Vestry obviously took umbrage to the part of the proposal where Christ Church had named the Reverend Taylor Willis as rector of the combined church. Bishop Thomson went on to say that he had met with both Reverend Willis and Reverend Jones and he was convinced that Reverend Jones had not taken offense to the proposal. Although the St. Andrew's resolution was very direct, he urged the Vestry of Christ Church to rescind the motion of November 17 and to continue the work of the merger committee. The Christ Church Vestry immediately rescinded the motion.

As it turned out, the Vestry of St. Andrew's was also meeting on the evening of November 19, 1934. Bishop Thomson telephoned them and inquired if they were willing for him to join their meeting for the purpose of updating them on the actions by the Vestry of Christ Church. Christ Church Vestry had unanimously approved the merger of the three churches with Reverend Willis and Reverend Jones serving as associate rectors of the combined church and Reverend Jones as the minister in charge of St. Andrew's Church. He wanted to give them his views. He also asked them not to take any action on the merger.

During the talks at St. Andrew's, Bishop Thomson stated that canonically there could not be equal associate rectors of a church. St. Andrew's then decided that they would support Reverend Willis as the rector of Christ Church and that Reverend Jones as the associate rector and minister in charge of St. Andrews. With this, it appeared that St. Andrew's was agreeable to the merger of the three churches.

At the annual Congregational Meeting of Christ Church on December 10, 1934, the merger of the three

Ghent Episcopal churches was approved by a vote of 104 to 25. St. Luke's congregation met on December 16, 1934 and the merger was approved by a vote of 167 to 105. The merger of the three churches was agreed to occur on June 1, 1935, the date of Dean Peacock's resignation as Rector of Christ Church.

Dean Peacock's final service as rector was broadcast over radio station WTAR. His tenure in Norfolk had been one marked by controversy. Not only had he been involved in the Lindbergh kidnapping saga, he also had been the local leader of many liberal causes including Sunday motion pictures.

Consolidation of the three churches occurred on June 2, 1935 at the 11 a.m. service. The officiant at the service was Bishop Thomson and the celebrant was the Reverend Norman E. Taylor, executive secretary of the Diocese of Southern Virginia. The sermon was preached by the Right Reverend Philip Cook, Bishop of Delaware and the president of the National Council of Episcopal Churches.

Under the agreement between the three churches, the merged church would be known as Christ & St. Luke's, and it no longer used the system of pew rents. For the members of the Christ Church congregation who had sat in the same seats for years (and for some, decades), this would be a huge change. Beverly Dabney recalled "deciding where to sit that first Sunday after the merger—to avoid trespassing on some Christ Church member's accustomed pew."

Many years later, Alex Grice, who was a child when the churches merged, remembered being overwhelmed by the size of the church. He recalled "It was such a contrast. St. Luke's was anything but Gothic. It was sort of overwhelming to go into that big, big church."

In September 1935, the St. Luke's building on Colonial Avenue was sold to the Glad Tidings Church. Glad Tidings had been organized just the prior year and was worshiping in a tabernacle tent at 33rd Street and DeBree Avenue.

Dean Peacock returned to England. On January 18, 1936, he was appointed as the Vicar of St. Barnabas Church in Derbyshire, England.

CHAPTER 8

Christ & St. Luke's Parish

B Y 1936, the former rectory had become the Guild House and was used for various church functions as well as providing Diocesan offices. The same year, the Rector Willis believed the church had been combined long enough to talk about the expansion of the parish house. In what has been a familiar refrain through the years, he deemed the parish house, built in 1919, "scattered and desultory accommodations for the church school were unsatisfactory and inadequate to present demands and the

The Guild House is pictured in the distance as the church begins to rise. The black splotch is probably a porch and a tree. Picture is courtesy of Christ & St. Luke's archives.

anticipated growth of the school; that the present second floor assembly Hall was inaccessible, difficult and unsafe to access and too remote from the kitchen facilities and the Guild Hall to provide accommodations for serving food to a large gathering."

His vision was to build a new building which would run adjacent to Pelham Place between the Parish House and Boissevain Avenue. The Vestry affirmed the vision and agreed to build an addition with a cost not to exceed $50,000. It was proposed that the building would be named for Bishop Arthur S. Lloyd, one of the previous rectors of St. Luke's Church. Frank R. Watson, architect for Christ Church, was hired for the design of the building. Financing would be from the church's capital fund which had been acquired in the merger with St. Luke's. One of the oddities of Virginia statues is that the court would have to agree to liquidate the church's investments for this purpose. As the Great Depression dragged on, plans to build a new parish house were postponed indefinitely in March 1937.

The Vestry minutes from November 1937 clearly reflect the difficult times for the church. In 1934, the last year in which the three churches operated separately, total revenues were $44,603.77. For 1936, the total contributions for the combined church had declined 22% to $36,725.60.

Another topic of conversation was the need for a new Rectory. One of the properties under consideration was the former home of Mr. Dillard located at 548 Mowbray Arch which was for sale for $8,000. The property needed repairs at an estimated cost of $1,000. The Vestry decided not to purchase the property. Within a couple of months, a new proposal for the purchase of this property was made based upon the exchange of a portion of the property where St. Luke's had been located on Colonial Avenue.

One of the exciting events for Christ & St. Luke's parishioners was the invitation by the Archbishop of York to the church's curate, the Reverend James DeWolf Perry, Jr. to be his chaplain at the coronation of King George VI in England. Perry was the son of the Right Reverend James DeWolf Perry, the seventh Bishop of Rhode Island and the eighteenth Presiding Bishop of the Episcopal Church in the United States. In 1930, the Right Reverend Perry had delivered the farewell sermon at the Lambeth Conference, the meeting of all Bishops in the Anglican Communion every ten years.

From the time of the combination of the three churches, it was always envisioned that St. Andrew's Church would separate from the combined church when finances allowed. In 1938 and 1939, St. Andrew's was able to pay all of its expenses and requested that a separate financial report be published in the *Jamestown Cross*. Additionally, St. Andrew's requested that a separate treasurer be maintained for the congregation. Movement to separate the St. Andrew's congregation from that of Christ & St. Luke's moved rapidly. On January 24, 1940, the Vestry of Christ & St. Luke's approved the separation. The Vestry minutes of February 14, 1940, reflect a written request by a committee of those worshipping at St. Andrew's for a petition to the Diocesan Convention to become a separate parish. The Diocesan Convention approved the separation later that year.

In February 1941, Reverend Willis again brought up the need for a new parish house. At the May 1941 Vestry meeting, a report recommended the construction of the building. There was barely a quorum at the meeting and apparently there was some opposition. At the June 1941 meeting, the majority of the Vestry opposed the construction of Lloyd Hall and Reverend Willis withdrew his request.

Until 1945, the niches in the Selden Chapel reredos had remained empty with the exception of the Angel Gabriel. The niches would be filled with St. Hilda (Abbess of

Whitby), St. Anne (mother of Mary), St. Elizabeth (mother of John the Baptist) and Matoaka, the American Indian Princess (also known as Pocohantas). At the center of the reredos would be the statue of the Virgin Mary which would be returned from the Norfolk Museum of Arts and Sciences (now Chrysler Museum). The Angel Gabriel would be placed in the stone lectern in the Selden Chapel.

On April 17, 1945, Christ & St. Luke's hosted the consecration of Reverend Bravid Washington Harris, the first bishop for the Missionary District of Liberia. The Right Reverend Harris, originally from Warrenton, North Carolina, had been the rector of Grace Episcopal Church, Norfolk, for nineteen years. During that time, he was active in the Norfolk community serving on many

Reredos in the Selden Chapel. From left to right: St. Hilda, St. Elizabeth, the Virgin Mary, St. Monica, and Pocohantas. To the far left is St. Perpetua and to the far right is St. Blandina. Photo courtesy of Rick Voight

Clergy in procession entering Christ & St. Luke's for the ordination of Reverend Harris. Notice that the church is covered with ivy. Photo courtesy of Sargeant Memorial Collection, Borjes Collection, Slover Library

boards, the Diocese of Southern Virginia and the National Church. He was consecrated bishop by the Right Reverend St. George Tucker, Presiding Bishop, the Right Reverend Edwin A. Pennick, the Bishop of North Carolina, and the Right Reverend William A. Brown, the Bishop of Southern Virginia. When the Right Reverend Harris died in 1965, his burial service was held in the Cathedral of St. Peter & St. Paul (National Cathedral) with interment in Arlington Cemetery.

Since its founding in the 1890s, Ghent had been a thriving neighborhood. The military expansion created by World War II negatively impacted the neighborhood as many homes took boarders or became multiple family houses, and temporary military housing was erected on the grounds of the Chrysler Museum. The neighborhood, traditionally a residential area, saw some commercial encroachment further changing the community dynamics.

By the end of World War II, approximately 5% of Norfolk's land area was high-density slums containing about 14% of the population. Downtown Norfolk was being choked by the surrounding poverty-stricken neighborhoods. Utilizing federal funds, city leaders embraced an initiative to clear the area of Monticello and Brambleton avenues, and constructed the lower density public housing developments of Young Park and Tidewater Park.

With the return of servicemen after World War II, there was a pent-up demand for housing and many people desired suburbia with large lots and new homes. As residents left the Ghent neighborhood, many church members transferred to new church homes. Christ & St. Luke's was also impacted by the facilities which, for years had been inadequate. For the next half century, church leadership would struggle with the double whammies of an increasingly secular society and flight from the city core.

During the Great Depression, Christ & St. Luke's shared the Guild House with the Diocese of Southern Virginia, which paid $50 per month as a maintenance fee to the church. This arrangement was meant to benefit both the Diocese as well as the parish. By 1949, the arrangement became the focus of the Vestry as part of a discussion about the need for additional space for the church. An assessment of the church property indicated that the church needed additional office space and identified that the Guild House could meet this need.

There were also some members of the Vestry who thought the time had come for the church to complete the long sought-after addition to the physical plant of the church. They noted that other churches in Norfolk had embarked on building programs and that Christ & St. Luke's was losing parishioners, particularly those with young children, due to the dated and insufficient facilities.

At the April 1949 Vestry meeting, a building committee

was formed consisting of three Vestry members and three men from the congregation. An advisory committee was also formed consisting of three women. The Vestry also approved a capital campaign to build the new facility.

Although the church had plans designed for an addition to the facilities in the 1930s, the design which integrated the building aesthetically with the church proper caused the construction costs to be excessive. As part of their due diligence, the Vestry explored the possibility of buying a house at Mowbray Arch and Fairfax Avenue to be used as the parish house. As this plan became known in the congregation, the Vestry received a large number of letters expressing opposition to the idea of purchasing the house, and this plan was soon abandoned.

Over the next year, the Vestry began to formulate how a new building could meet with the needs of the church. The wish list was long and included an auditorium seating 250 adults, a kitchen capable of providing meals for 200 people, laundry facilities for the cleaning of choir and clergy vestments, a secondary meeting room of about 1,200 square feet, a choir rehearsal and robing room, and a game room for children. They also wanted the exterior to be made of stone to match the church. The plan also focused on utilization of the Guild House to meet the needs of the parish. This included using the basement of the Guild House for the Boy Scouts, the Cub Pack, and the Sea Scouts. The main floor of the Guild House would provide office space as well as space for the Women's Auxiliary.

At a special meeting of the Vestry on July 7, 1950, a plan for the building was approved by the Vestry. The estimated cost of the building was $92,000. Additionally, the Vestry approved an upgrade of the heating system ($7,000) and new lights for the church ($3,500). This plan was affirmed by the congregation on October 8, 1950 by a vote of 220 in favor and 20 opposed.

Construction of the building which would be called Lloyd Hall was begun in late 1950. The Diocese of Southern Virginia continued to occupy the Guild House. In April 1951 the Diocese space was confined to the second and third floors of the Guild House and the rent was increased. By October 1951, the work was substantially complete. Although the dedication of the building wouldn't occur until in early 1952 when everything was finished, the Vestry approved the use of the building for the church bazaar and for Sunday School.

The keynote speaker at the dedication of Lloyd Hall was the Reverend Dr. Churchill J. Gibson, the rector of St. James Church in Richmond and the son-in-law of the Reverend Arthur Lloyd for whom the building was named. Lloyd Hall provided Sunday School classrooms in the basement. The first floor didn't look like it does today. In many ways, it resembled the second floor of the parish house. It was a large room with a stage located on the end nearest the parish house. The kitchen was located in a connector with the Guild House. The second floor room was a projection room. The wall, which defined a hallway, the bathrooms, and the kitchen were added at a later date.

Dr. Taylor Willis, rector of St. Luke's Church and Christ & St. Luke's Church since 1932, announced his retirement effective December 31, 1953. The Reverend Peyton R. Williams was called rector of the church. A native of Richmond, Virginia, Reverend Williams had served St. Mary's and St. John's Churches in Georgetown for five years before accepting a call to Christ Church in Georgetown. At the time of his call to Christ & St. Luke's Church, Reverend Williams was the rector of St. George's Church in Nashville, Tennessee. He had been at St. George's Church since its founding in 1947 and had been involved in the construction of the original church.

In the late 1950s and early 1960s, a trend of televising church services swept across the country. Christ & St. Luke's followed First Presbyterian Church and Freemason Street Baptist Church in broadcasting services for a six-month period by WTAR-TV (Channel 3). To accommodate the telecast, a special platform was built on the Epistle side of the church and special lighting was added. In earlier decades, services had been broadcast by radio from the church.

During a violent thunderstorm on July 7, 1955, a lightning bolt struck the tower. Thankfully, the tower was made of stone rather than of wood. The church could have gone up in flames just as the original Christ Church did in 1827 and St. Luke's did in 1921. The force of the lightning bolt caused a spire measuring 3 feet long and 1½ feet in depth to fall from the tower to earth creating a 6-inch deep hole. No one was walking under the tower when the spire came crashing down. The firm of Overmyer and Ennis, stonemasons, was hired to replace the spire. After making the stub of the spire ready for the replacement, three sections of Indiana limestone with a total length of 9 feet, 6 inches and weighing approximately 5,000 pounds were lifted and secured into place. At 6:45 a.m. on July 15, 1966, lightning again struck the church tower, causing a 6-foot finial to come crashing down to earth.

In the late 1950s, the second area to face the bulldozer was the Atlantic City area of Norfolk. Unlike the earlier redevelopment effort, there was no attempt to provide replacement housing for the displaced residents. Many fled to East Ghent, the area surrounded by Olney Road, Colonial Avenue, Granby Street and 21st Street. While the redevelopment of Atlantic City continued, Ghent continued its downward trend.

Grover Oberle seated at the console of Christ & St. Luke's. Photo courtesy of William McIntosh.

AFTER 30 YEARS as organist and choirmaster of Christ Church, George Vail announced his retirement effective November 30, 1958. After a search, Grover Oberle was hired. He had grown up in New York City and had sung at St. Thomas Church as a child. He later was an assistant to Dr. T. Tertius Noble, who had instituted the choir of men and boys and started the choir school at St. Thomas, 5th Avenue. At the time of his calling to Christ & St. Luke's, Mr. Oberle was the organist at Emmanuel Church in Boston.

Oberle had a vision for a choir school patterned after St. Thomas Church where musical training would be part of the daily curriculum. At the time of Oberle's arrival in Norfolk, the choir of men and boys had fourteen boys between the ages of nine and fourteen. As part of his initiative, Oberle established five weekly practice sessions for the boy choristers—an hour of personal instruction on Monday, an hour on Tuesdays and Saturdays with just the boys, an hour rehearsal with the men and boys on Wednesdays, and a forty-minute rehearsal just before the church service.

In his first year at Christ & St. Luke's, Oberle also started The Cantata Chorus, a mixed ensemble dedicated to performing sacred choral pieces. The first performance was Bach's *St. John's Passion* during Holy Week 1959. Oberle was the vice president of the American Guild of Organists and a member of the editorial board that created *The American Organist* magazine.

OVER THE YEARS, the American taste in organ sound had changed from the orchestral sound to one more resembling the organs played during the time of J. S. Bach. Called "American Classic", organs in this style had a brighter sound. As part of the agreement with Oberle to become the organist was the replacement of the Austin organ. The old organ was over fifty years old, which is about the life span of an organ before a major renovation is needed, and this organ was showing its age. A note in the Parish Bulletin said that the organ was being "held together by string, scotch tape, paper-clips, etc."

The church selected Casavant Organs of Canada to build a 67-rank, three-manual organ at a cost of $71,000. Installed in 1963, the organ was used by Oberle to play the dedication recital on September 29. At the dedication of the organ, the choir sang "Behold, the tabernacle of God is with men" by Healey Willan and Ralph Vaughn Williams' *Festival Te Deum*. The festivities also included a dedication recital played by Fernando Germani, the organist at St. Peter's in Rome. Germani had studied under Italian composer Ottorino Respighi. The concert reportedly drew 1,300 people to the church.

As the Ghent area continued to deteriorate, Norfolk Mayor Pretlow Darden stated, "We have slums developing in the Ghent section where some of our finest homes are located; unless we find some means to deal with the problem, the area will go into slums within a year or so." Christ & St. Luke's future was, in large part, dependent upon whether or not the Ghent area of Norfolk experienced a rebirth.

Thankfully, in April 1961, the City Council instructed Norfolk Housing and Redevelopment to develop a Ghent Conservation Plan. A year later, residents formed the Ghent Neighborhood League. In 1964, Ghent was declared a conservation area which made federally insured loans available for the rehabilitation of homes in the area. The renaissance of Ghent was set in motion.

The exterior lighting of the tower in September, 1963, was through a gift by a parishioner. This has become a familiar sight in Norfolk. It is particularly comforting to those who are nearby in Sentara Norfolk General Hospital.

This church has often been a place where the community has gathered during times of stress. Christ & St. Luke's opened its doors to a community in shock and grief following the assassination of President John F. Kennedy in November 1963.

Christ & St. Luke's endowment was established by parishioners January, 1964, to support the facilities of the church. The endowment was crucial during the difficult economic times for the church in the later 1980s and early 1990s. In 1974 funds were given by Mr. & Mrs. George

Curtis, Jr. to support Christian Education. The Vestry decided to have the funds administered by the trustees of the endowment. Today the endowment is composed of several different funds thanks to the generosity of parishioners and the growth of the investments.

At the 1964 Diocesan Convention, the issue of women serving on Vestries was raised but failed to reach the required two-thirds majority. At the 1965 Diocesan Convention, the topic was once again raised. Since in the 1964 vote, they had secured a majority of the votes but not the two-thirds required for passing on the first ballot, only a majority of votes in support of women on the Vestry was required. This time the resolution passed. Mrs. Virgil (Connie) Laws was the first woman to serve on the Vestry of Christ & St. Luke's Church beginning in 1970.

BY THE MID-1960s, the old Christ Church on Freemason Street was showing its age. Many in Norfolk wanted to preserve the iconic structure. After Christ Church moved to Ghent, the property was sold to the Annunciation Greek Orthodox Cathedral in 1911. When the Greek Orthodox Church moved to a new facility on Granby Street, the building became the home of Sweet Precious Daddy Grace's United House of Prayer in 1955. Its columns were painted red, white, and blue.

Sweet Precious Daddy Grace's United House of Prayer began in the northeast. Daddy Grace first visited Norfolk in 1926 and by 1930, he had established his first United House of Prayer in Norfolk on 17th Street. Daddy Grace acquired the former Christ Church in 1955 and his congregation worshiped there until 1960. At one point the church had over 10,000 members in Norfolk. At his death in 1960, there were approximately 350 United House of Prayer churches throughout the United States. Daddy Grace also built

Grace Village Apartments in Norfolk where he maintained an apartment.

After Daddy Grace's congregation left the church, the property was acquired by Norfolk Housing & Redevelopment for $50,500 and it was boarded up. The Victorian stained glass windows were removed and stored in the basement of the Norfolk Housing & Redevelopment Authority. Five of the stained glass windows were purchased in 1982 by the First Baptist Church of Lynnhaven.

BY 1965 THERE SEEMED to be a groundswell of interest in this historic part of the cityscape. Various parties were interested in buying and restoring old Christ Church including the Norfolk Historical Society which started a fund raising campaign of $100,000. The movement to save the old building gained steam later in 1966 when the Preservation of Virginia Antiquities and the Junior Chamber of Commerce joined with the Norfolk Historical Society in a fund-raising effort. Preservationists hopes soared when an engineering survey pronounced the building to be "sound, impressive and worthy of preservation." The chair of the Old Christ Church Preservation Committee was Robert M. Hughes, III, a member of Christ & St. Luke's.

In early April 1967, C. W. Tazewell, executive director of the Norfolk Historical Society, advanced a plan to purchase the old church and to use the facility for a mid-size auditorium which could be leased to performing groups. There was also a developer interested in buying the property. The developer planned to restore the exterior of the property while the interior would be converted to offices. The estimated cost of purchasing and rehabbing the property had grown to $200,000. The Norfolk Housing & Redevelopment Authority increased the pressure for action when they set a deadline for the purchase of the property

Situated on a stream, the stairs from the Selden Chapel were sinking in 1966. E. T. Gresham was called in to make repairs, which included sinking new pilings. Photo courtesy of E. T. Gresham Company

at the end of the month. When the deadline came, the Norfolk Historical Society had raised pledges of $50,000 of the needed $200,000. The plans of the developer didn't materialize either.

The years dragged on for the old church and the interest in buying it continued to wax and wane. In 1971, the church along with Freemason Street Baptist Church and the Willoughby-Baylor house were placed on the Virginia landmarks list by the State's Historic Landmark Commission. Placement on the Virginia Historic Landmark Commission did not have the same gravitas as being listed on the National Register of Historic Places. The national register can, by law, protect a building from demolition or substantial structural change.

The day after the church was listed on the Virginia Historic Landmark Commission, strong winds blew off the pine and oak cupola which had been damaged by winds earlier in the year. With termites ravaging the building and it beginning to fall apart, the end was not far away. Norfolk Housing & Redevelopment Authority again set a deadline for someone to express interest in buying and renovating the building for early December 1972. Although the Norfolk Housing & Redevelopment Authority was willing to sell the property for $1, they required that any purchaser have the financial wherewithal to restore it. By this time, the estimated cost to renovate the property as a church had increased to $350,000 and for another purpose, $150,000. Once again, there were no interested parties in purchasing the old building. The end came in early January 1973 when the building was demolished.

REVEREND WILLIAMS accepted a call as the rector of St. Matthew's Episcopal Church in Wheeling, West Virginia and left the church on January 1, 1967. His replacement, the Reverend A. Heath Light, was called as the rector a year later and was installed on January 10, 1968. The service included a choral evensong and the festivities concluded with a reception in Lloyd Hall.

In June 1967, the choir joined forces with WHRO-TV to make a documentary on *The Art of Plainsong*. The documentary traces the musical heritage of the pre-Renaissance period. A portion of the filming of the documentary was done in the church with some portions being filmed at the WHRO-TV studios.

COMMUNITY OUTREACH has long been a cornerstone of Christ & St. Luke's Church. As the neighborhood surrounding it deteriorated, the church continued to be a beacon to the neighborhood. In June 1971, Christ & St. Luke's was the driving force behind the founding of the Norfolk Free Clinic. This clinic was located in the basement of Lloyd Hall and was staffed by volunteer doctors. To fund this outreach, Christ & St Luke's founded the Ghent Arts Festival. In 1984, the arts festival was acquired by Hope House as their primary fundraiser. Today, Hope House runs the Stockley Gardens Art Festival in both the spring and the fall attracting 50,000 visitors. Christ & St. Luke's continues to use the Stockley Gardens Art Festival as a community outreach program, opening their doors for tours. The Norfolk Free Clinic remained at Christ & St. Luke's for several years until better facilities were donated by a retired doctor.

Kirking of the Tartan

Edward B. McCaskey, a member of Christ & St. Luke's, and Charles McDuffie approached Reverend Light about establishing a "Kirking of the Tartan" service. According to tradition, the Kirking traces its roots back to the Jacobean

Bagpiper. Photo courtesy of Rick Voight

Rebellion in 1745. Prince Charles Edward Stuart tried to reestablish the House of Stuart as the monarchy for Britain. After he was defeated, Britain passed the Act of Proscription 1746 which forbade the Scottish from wearing their traditional highland dress. The Scots responded by taking pieces of their tartans to church for blessing.

In America, the Kirking of the Tartan was started by Reverend Peter Marshall, the pastor at the New York Avenue Presbyterian Church in Washington, D.C., during World War II as a celebration of Scottish heritage. Reverend Marshall wanted to instill a sense of pride in Scottish-Americans with the hope they would join the fight in Britain. Originally the Kirking was held in Presbyterian churches but in 1954, it was held at the National Cathedral.

The Kirking of the Tartan became a Christ & St. Luke's tradition beginning in 1978. The highlight of the service was the procession of bagpipes and drums into and out of the church and the blessing of the tartans. It became a very popular service appealing to many outside of the parish.

Reverend Light would serve as the rector of Christ & St. Luke's until 1979 when he was elected Bishop of Southwest Virginia.

Christ & St. Luke's Church was added to the list of Virginia Historical Landmarks Register in April 1979.

When The Williams School expanded in 1985, the school's annex was razed to make space for a new facility which impacted the second, third, and fourth grades. Freddie Ewell, the church's Junior Warden, arranged for two unused rooms at Christ & St. Luke's to be renovated. During the six months of construction, the Williams School buses would transport second and fourth grade children to Christ & St. Luke's who were met at the door by the rector, the Reverend Jim Samuel.

The Casavant organ was expanded in 1984 to include a 68th rank, the Trompette de Fete, in honor of Oberle's 25th anniversary.

In 1990, the church was used for the filming of the movie *Twilight Blue.* The producers, Shuki Levi and Debbie Shelton, had a connection with Norfolk. Shelton had grown up in Norfolk, graduated from Norview High School and attended Old Dominion University in pre-med. Angry at a boyfriend, Shelton entered the Miss Virginia contest and won. From there she went to New York to begin her theatrical career which included a three-year stint as a mistress to J.R. Ewing on *Dallas.*

The plot of *Twilight Blue* was a woman attending a church service spotting a man she had earlier seen leaving the scene of a crime. Nearly 5,000 area citizens participated in the filming, primarily as extras during the church services and joined in singing the hymn "Jesus, Lover of My Soul." The Cantata Chorus played the role of the church choir.

In September 1990, Charlie Sheen and a film crew came to Norfolk to shoot the opening scene of *Navy Seals* at Christ & St. Luke's Church.

Blessing of the Animals

The Blessing of the Animals has been a special service at Christ & St. Luke's. Over the years, it has been held in the Lychgate Garden or in the church either as part of the regular service or as a separate service. When animals were included as a part of the regular worship, they were, for the most part, remarkably well behaved.

An animal being blessed by the Rev. Canon Win Lewis.

Dr. Allen Shaffer seated at the organ console. Photo courtesy of Rick Voight

One year, a parishioner brought a favorite bird for the Blessing of the Animals, which fortunately, was held inside. Lo and behold, the bird escaped from its cage and enjoyed soaring around the interior of the building. Allen Shaffer, seated at the console, put sheet music over the top of his head as the bird flew through the choir portion of the church.

Music at Christ & St. Luke's

After a thirty-year tenure at the organ console of Christ & St. Luke's Church, Grover Oberle retired. He was succeeded by Dr. Allen Shaffer who had been the church's assistant organist since 1982. Dr. Shaffer grew up in western Pennsylvania and studied at the Oberlin College Conservatory of Music and Syracuse University. After receiving his PhD from the University of Michigan, Shaffer relocated to Norfolk to join the music faculty at

Norfolk State University, a position he held for twenty-seven years. In addition to being the organist at Christ & St. Luke's, Dr. Shaffer was the principal keyboard artist for the Virginia Symphony (1974-1984) and was a founder of Norfolk Chamber Consort.

THROUGHOUT THE YEARS, music has been one of the mainstays of Christ & St. Luke's. With a changing of the times which found young boys more interested in sports than music, the choir once again became mixed voices. Under Dr. Allen Shaffer, who succeeded Grover Oberle as organist and choir director, the church hosted a visiting men and girls' choir from St. David's Cathedral in Wales in October 1998. The choir director from Wales suggested that Christ & St. Luke's Choir come to St. David's. This began a series of choir tours outside of Hampton Roads.

By the early 1990s, the Casavant organ was showing its age. It was experiencing frequent mechanical failures caused by age and the heat and humidity of Tidewater summers. Additionally, there had been a change in the tonal qualities desired in church organs. In the middle of a service in 1995, the organ completely failed. The choir had processed in to the sounds of the organ, and left to the sounds of a piano.

A committee chaired by Mrs. Connie Laws and Mrs. Rachel Hopkins was developed to oversee the restoration project. Orgues Letourneau of St. Hyacinthe, Quebec, was hired in March, 1996, not only to renovate the organ but also to expand it to 77 ranks with a total of 4,197 pipes. The renovated organ was returned to Norfolk in November, 1996, and a special evening liturgy was held on Friday, December 13, 1996.

Staying close to home, the choir sang a choral evensong at St. James in Richmond, Virginia and Old Donation Church in Virginia Beach. Following a visit from Dr.

Christ & St. Luke's Choir. Easter, 2016.
Photo courtesy of Rick Voight

Gere Hancock, organist and choir master at St. Thomas Church, New York, the choir sang the Eucharist service at St. Thomas. After a series of fundraisers, the choir crossed over the pond to England and Wales performing a concert and choral evensong at St. David's in 2000. The trip was a mixture of singing and touring, including a brief trip to Ireland. On the trip back to London, the choir sang concerts at Salisbury Cathedral and Southwark Cathedral in London.

A second choir tour to England in 2002 began with a concert at St. Giles Cathedral in Edinburgh, Scotland. On July 4, the choir traveled to the small town of Howarth, stopping for lunch at a lunchroom in the town where the tables were decorated with the American flag. Arriving at St. Michael's, the choir noticed that the church was flying the Stars and Stripes from the flag post atop the tower. Late that afternoon, the choir sang a concert at St. Michael's Church in Howarth. When the choir was leaving, they were

107

accorded the privilege of lowering the American flag from the tower. The choir also sang at William Shakespeare's church, Holy Trinity in Stratford-upon-Avon, and St. Sepulchres in London.

A third choir trip to England in 2006 was the most ambitious of the various tours under Dr. Allen Shaffer. The choir was the "choir in residence" at Worcester Cathedral. In England, many cathedral churches have visiting choirs perform the duties of the cathedral choir during the summer months. The mornings and early afternoons were spent touring various locations in Worcester, York, and the Cotswalds. When they returned around 3 p.m. in the afternoon, there would be a rehearsal followed by tea (and coffee) and cookies. At the appointed hour, the choir would process into Worcester Cathedral to sing a choral evensong.

With the retirement of Dr. Shaffer in 2012, Kevin Kwan assumed the mantle of organist and Director of Music after an exhaustive nationwide search. Mr. Kwan holds performance degrees from the University of California at San Diego and the Cleveland Institute of Music. After completion of his studies, he served as the organ scholar

Kevin Kwan became the Director of Music and Organist in October, 2013. Photo courtesy of Rick Voight

Christ & St. Luke's choir, 2016. Photo courtesy of Kevin Kwan

at Gloucester Cathedral in England. Most recently, he was the Assistant Organist at St. Thomas Church 5th Avenue, New York City.

THE TRADITION OF TOURING continues for the choir. Under Mr. Kwan's leadership, the choir returned to St. Thomas Church 5th Avenue in July 2015 to once again sing the Eucharist. In the afternoon, the choir sang a choral evensong at St. John the Divine Cathedral. In 2016, the choir was the "choir in residence" at Gloucester and Norwich cathedrals in England where they sang three Choral Eucharists and nine Choral Evensongs.

CHAPTER 9

The Church as Storyteller

W HEN GOTHIC CHURCHES were built in Europe and England during the Middle Ages, books were extremely rare as they were hand copied. Additionally, the vast majority of the people were illiterate. Usually the only copy of the Bible and the Prayer Book was used by the priest. The detail in a Gothic church tells the story of the church.

That is true at Christ & St. Luke's. Even though the congregation of Christ Church was well educated, the church was designed to be true to its Gothic roots. Everything in the church building represents a story.

The story-telling begins before you enter the church. There are four statues on the exterior—St. Peter and St. Paul at the front door and St. Stephen above the side door of the Selden Chapel. In the peak of the nave facing Olney Road is Jesus Christ.

St. Peter is on the left hand side of the main entrance. Also known as Simon Peter, he

Christ as the Good Shepherd stands in the center of the main reredos in Christ & St. Luke's Church.

was one of the Twelve Apostles and a leader in the early Christian Church. It was Peter who denied knowing Jesus three times before Christ's crucifixion. St. Peter was very influential in the early church and is considered to have been the founder along with St. Paul of the church in Rome. Roman Catholics consider him to be the first Pope.

During the early days of Christianity, **St. Paul** worked for the destruction of the new religion and actively persecuted the followers of Jesus. On the road to Damascus, he was blinded by the resurrected Jesus for three days resulting in his conversion. After regaining his sight, St. Paul began to preach that Jesus was the Son of God. Although fourteen of the twenty-seven books of the New Testament have been attributed to St. Paul, only seven are undisputed. The remainder are believed to have been written by his followers using letters he had written. His epistles are the foundation of the Roman, Protestant and Eastern Orthodox churches. St. Paul has been credited with the theology of atonement. He taught that Christians are redeemed from sin through Jesus' death and resurrection. His statue is on the right hand side of the main entrance.

St. Stephen, whose statue is over the exterior door on Stockley Gardens, was considered the first martyr of the church. He was a Hellenistic Jew who sought to improve life for the Greek-speaking Jewish widows by distributing food and other charitable aid to them. His preaching was in conflict with that of other Jewish groups. He was accused of blasphemy, taken in front of a Jewish court, and having been found guilty, was stoned to death.

Building design

The design of the building is divided into three sections —the nave where the congregation sits, the chancel (or choir) which is between the nave and the sanctuary, and the sanctuary where the Eucharist is performed. There is symbolism behind the choir being higher than the nave and the sanctuary being the highest of all. The nave represents the life of this world. The chancel which includes the pulpit and the lectern for instruction and the choir for the enhancement of worship. The sanctuary connotes God's presence through the Sacrament of Eucharist.

In Gothic churches, the church faced east so that the sanctuary is at the east end of the building symbolically representing the second coming of Christ. Another reason for this is that the rising sun would illuminate the windows which were designed to tell a story. Although Christ & St. Luke's faces geographically north, the adherence to a church facing liturgically east is why the aisle nearest to the parish house (which is really the east aisle) is called the south aisle.

The flood of light through the windows represents God's grace. In a medieval church, the light which flowed through the clerestory windows helped the people to forget, at least momentarily, their harsh lives. It gave a respite from their everyday world and pointed towards a better world.

Stained glass windows

The stained glass windows at Christ & St. Luke's are the primary tellers of the Bible stories. They were crafted by the firm of Mayer & Company of Munich, Germany which has a long-storied history. Wanting to revitalize the medieval building trades, Joseph Gabriel Mayer started the firm in 1847 as the "Institute for Christian Art." About 1860, the firm began working in stained glass. They were involved in the stained glass at Cologne and Regensberg Cathedrals. Under Franz Borgias Mayer, the founder's son, the company expanded to over 500 employees and maintained offices in London, England, and New York. Franz Mayer was heavily involved in the crafting of the windows at Christ & St. Luke's. Frank Watson, the architect of the building, described the windows as "the best windows Mayer ever made."

The clerestory (upper) windows at Christ & St. Luke's are replicas of the clerestory windows at Cologne Cathedral.

In the tower vestibule is a stained glass window of **St. John the Baptist** preaching.

In the east vestibule is a stained glass window of **St. Paul**'s sermon on Mars Hill.

The Great West window reflects the tales of the Old Testament. It is 11 feet by 25 feet and has five lancets and twenty panels. The panels include the Garden of Eden, Cain and Abel, The Flood, Abraham and the Angelic Visitants, Sacrifice of Isaac, Melchizdek, Barter and Sale of Joseph, Jacob going into Egypt, the Passover, Exodus, Crossing the Red Sea, Water from the Rock, Serpent on the Pole, manna in the Wilderness, Moses and the Law, David the King, the Scapegoat. The great prophesies are the Suffering Servant, Blessing of Baalam, and Blessing of Judah.

The Te Deum window is over the high altar. The five lower panels on the Te Deum window tell the story of Jesus' crucifixion and resurrection. The one on the lower left is the picture of the crowd choosing Barabbas over Jesus to be saved from crucifixion. The next one is of Jesus in the Garden of Gethsemane with the Cup being offered to Him in when he says "Nevertheless not My will but Thy will be done." The center panel is the Crucifixion. The next panel toward the right on the Epistle-side is the coming out of the tomb. The last is the Ascension. The main section portrays Christ enthroned in glory surrounded by the Sages, Prophets, Apostles, Martyrs of the Holy Church throughout the world and the glorious heavenly hosts. Note that all of the figures are looking toward Christ.

113

THE WINDOWS in the Selden Chapel are from the life of Christ.

The Annunciation window. The angel Gabriel, appears to Mary announcing that she has been chosen to be the mother of Jesus whose title would be "The Son of the Most High."

The Visitation window. Mary is told by an angel that her cousin, Elizabeth, is pregnant. Elizabeth pregnancy is miraculous—one very late in life, thought to be impossible. The child Elizabeth will bear is John the Baptist. The Gospel tells us that "when Elizabeth heard Mary's greeting, the child leaped in her womb," the first acknowledgement of who Jesus was born to be. Mary's response is to articulate the Magnificat, a Canticle said or sung at Evening Prayer and other appropriate times.

The Nativity window. This window tells the story of the birth of Jesus.

The Adoration of the Kings window. This window tells the story of the visit of the Magi to the Christ child bringing gifts of gold, frankincense, and myrrh. The Epiphany, the Manifestation of Christ to the Gentiles/the Visit of the Magi, bringing gifts of Gold, Frankincense, & Myrrh. This Festival was observed as early as the second century and is known by a variety of names including Epiphany and the Manifestation of Christ to the Gentiles.

The Presentation in the Temple window. Earlier called the Purification of St. Mary the Virgin or Candlemas, this Holy Day takes place on February 2. The Gospel account tells of Christ being presented to Simeon, a priest who received and dedicated Him to God, as mandated by the Law of Moses for the first born son.

Christ and the Doctors in the Temple window. Our Lord's parents had gone to Jerusalem for the Feast of the Passover. Jesus stayed behind to ask questions and listen to the Elders. When His mother takes Him to task for causing concern, he says those memorable words, "Wist ye not that I must be about my Father's business?"

Baptism window. This window, appropriately, is directly across from the Baptismal Font. It tells the story of Jesus' Baptism by John the Baptist.

THE SOUTH AISLE windows represent Christ's ministry. Starting at the back of the church:

The Miracle at Cana window. This window depicts our Lord's first miracle: the water turns into wine before one's very eyes. Young people seem especially delighted at such detail.

Christ and Nicodemus window. The right hand panel of this window portrays Nicodemus coming to Jesus by night and being told that "no-one can enter the kingdom of God without being born of water and Spirit." (Baptism) There is not consensus much less total agreement as to the Scripture applicable to the left side of the window.

The Return of the Prodigal Son window. This window is a depiction of the return of the prodigal son. The story is actually about the father, the intent of which is to remind us of the Heavenly Father who forever comes out to forgive us. Notice all of the main features of the piece: the bedraggled son, the elder brother, the robe, the ring, etc.

Transfiguration window. This window tells the story of Jesus accompanied by the Apostles Peter, James and John, ascending a mountain. While speaking with Moses and Elijah, Jesus was transfigured—he was radiant in glory.

Christ Blessing the Little Children window. This window is another connection to Holy Baptism, for as this Sacrament was celebrated using earlier Prayer Books, the lesson read was always the memorable one from St. Mark's Gospel, 10: 13-16: "People were bringing little children to Him in order that He might touch them; and the disciples spoke sternly to them. But when Jesus saw this, he was indignant and said to them, 'Let the little children come to me; do not stop them; for it is to such as these that the kingdom of God belongs. Truly, I tell you, whoever does not receive the kingdom of God as a little child will never enter it'." And he took them up in his arms, laid his hands on them, and blessed them."

Statuary

The statuary in the church convey the history of the church. At the high altar are figures in the early church and those important during the church's formation in America. The figures at the altar in the Selden Chapel represent women of significance. The statues which are atop the columns in the nave of the church are others of significance in history.

The four statues at the high altar on either side of the Newton Memorial Reredos are the four evangelists: St. Matthew (upper left), St. Mark (lower left), St. Luke (upper right) and St. John (lower right).

St. Matthew was called to be one of the twelve apostles while sitting in the tax collector's place. He was the author of the first Gospel having witnessed the Resurrection and Ascension of Christ.

St. Mark was the author of the second Gospel and founded the Church of Alexandria. He is frequently symbolized by a lion, a figure of courage and monarchy. Some legends say that when he was thrown to the lions instead of attacking him, they slept at his feet. Upon seeing this, the Romans released St. Mark from his imprisonment.

St. Luke has been credited with writing both the Gospel of St. Luke and the Acts of the Apostles. He is believed by many to have been a Greek physician although some believe he was a Hellenistic Jew. The Symbol of St. Luke is an ox frequently depicted with wings.

St. John and his brother, James, were among the first disciples called by Jesus. He was the author of the fourth Gospel and is believed to be the author of the Book of Revelation. His symbol as an evangelist is an eagle.

Anna the Prophetess' statue is located in the choir on the right side (as you face the altar). She was an aged Jewish woman who prophesied about Jesus. According to Jewish tradition, a child was brought to the temple on the fortieth day for purification. Anna who spent her days at the Temple in prayer was present at the Presentation of Jesus in the Temple. Upon seeing the Christ child, she saw what others could not. In a loud voice, she tells that this child would bring redemption to Israel.

Simeon is also located in the choir directly across from Anna the Prophetess. He was at the Temple when Jesus was brought by Mary and Joseph for purification.

Earlier Simeon had been visited by the Holy Spirit and told that he would not die until he had seen the Lord's Christ. Upon taking Jesus into his arms, he uttered a prayer which we know as the Nunc Dimittis. "Lord, now lettest thou thy servant depart in peace according to Thy word. For mine eyes have seen Thy salvation which Thou hast prepared before the face of all people; To be a light to lighten the Gentiles and to be the glory of Thy people Israel."

St. Peter, also known as Simon Peter, was one of the Twelve Apostles and a leader in the early Christian Church. It was Peter who denied knowing Christ three times before his crucifixion. St. Peter was very influential in the early church and is considered along with St. Paul to have been the founder of the church in Rome. Roman Catholics consider him to be the first Pope.

Irenaeus (early second century), was the Bishop of Lugdunum (now Lyon, France) and one of the great theologians of the early Church. His writings were important in the development of Christian theology especially in contrast to the Gnostics who had also developed a strong following. In a five-volume book, *Against Heresies,* Irenaeus refuted the Gnostic doctrine. Irenaeus emphasized traditional elements in the church, particularly the episcopate, Scripture and tradition.

Cyprian was an important early Christian writer and his works paralleled his ministry. He exhorted his followers to be charitable to the poor. He was also an active defender of the Christian faith. Born into a wealthy pagan family, Cyprian was baptized at age thirty-five and gave away a portion of his wealth to the poor. Shortly after his conversion to Christianity, Cyprian became bishop of Carthage. During his time as bishop, the Romans demanded that the Christians sacrifice to the pagan gods. In order to avoid persecution and probable execution, Cyprian went into hiding. During this period of persecution, many of Christians fell away from the faith and were referred to as lapsi (from which comes the term of lapsed Christians). In a second period of persecution, he refused to sacrifice to the pagan gods and reaffirmed his faith in Christ. After a year of banishment from Carthage, he was ordered to die by the sword to which he exclaimed, "Thanks be to God." His beheading was carried out in a public square.

At a young age, **Athanasius** was playing with some friends down by the seashore near the home of the Bishop of Alexandria. Watching the children play from a window, the Bishop noticed they were imitating the ritual of a Christian baptism. The Bishop sent for the boys and learned that Athanasius was acting as bishop in the make-believe baptisms. The Bishop of Alexandria decided to recognize the make-believe baptisms and encouraged the boys to pursue a religious career.

Athanasius was the first person to identify the twenty-seven books of the New Testament which continue in use today. He believed in what would later become the Trinity—God the Father, God the Son and God the Holy Spirit. When Emperor Constantine the Great summoned the 1,800 bishops to Nicea to bring peace to the church, they discussed, fought and finally hammered out the Nicene Creed. The basis for the Creed was *On the Incarnation* written by Athanasius.

John Chrysostom was known for his preaching and public speaking and for his denunciation of the abuse of authority by both church and political leaders. John was born in Antioch and his early education was by Libanius from whom John learned his oratory skills. Upon a deepening of his Christian faith, John Chrysostom studied theology. He lived for several years as a hermit during which time he committed the Bible to memory. He was ordained a deacon in 381 A.D. and a presbyter (preacher) in 385 A.D.

Known as "the greatest preacher in the early Church," his homilies are his greatest lasting legacy. Due to the efforts of stenographers, there are hundreds of his homilies that remain today. He frequently emphasized charitable giving and was concerned with the treatment of the poor. He put his words of concern for the poor into deeds with the founding of a series of hospitals in Constantinople for the poor. He was elected the Bishop of Constantinople in 397 A.D.

Augustine of Hippo was an early theologian and philosopher whose writings influenced the development of Western Christianity. He helped to formulate the doctrine of original sin and made contributions to the "just war" theory.

As a young man, Augustine of Hippo left the Christian faith to join the Manichaeism faith. Among the tenets of Manichaeism is the struggle between good and evil which contributed to his philosophy of original sin. After developing a skepticism towards Manichaeism, a meeting with St. Ambrose of Milan resulted in his re-embracing Christianity.

Although his original career was as a teacher in Carthage, Rome, and Milan, after his conversion to Christianity, he returned to the family home. After the death of his mother and his son, he sold everything except for his home, giving the proceeds to the poor. He converted his home into a monastery. Four years after being ordained, he became the Bishop of Hippo.

Gregory the Great was born into a wealthy Roman family with strong connections to the church. His third great grandfather was Pope Felix III, and his mother and two paternal aunts are honored in the Roman Catholic and Orthodox churches as saints.

By 590 the Lombards had overrun the majority of Italy. Rome was teeming with refugees and there wasn't enough food or other basic living necessities. The Roman Empire had collapsed and the seat of government, Constantinople, was unable to provide supplies to alleviate the suffering in Rome. By then a Bishop, Gregory began organizing the church for the relief of the poor.

Music has been a part of the church since the earliest of days, and by the fifth century, there were many forms of chanting. In his standardization of the liturgy, Gregory, known for his love of music, gathered various forms of chants and organized them for use in various services. Although the development of Gregorian chant from Roman and Gallican chants did not occur until the mid-eighth century, many point to the earlier efforts of Gregory to standardize the use of chants as the reason for the naming of the chant after him.

Starting on the bottom row of statues in the reredos working toward the right, the statues are as follows:

Bishop Samuel Seabury  was the first Bishop in the United States. After graduating from Yale College, he studied theology with his father, an Anglican priest. He also studied medicine in Edinburgh where, in 1753, he was ordained in the Church of England and returned to the colonies. Seabury remained loyal to Britain during the American Revolution. During the war, he was imprisoned for six weeks. After being released by the Patriots, he became the chaplain to the King's American Regiment. After the conclusion of the American Revolution, he was loyal to the new government.

He was elected Bishop by ten Episcopal clergy in 1783. Since there were no American Bishops, he sailed to England to be consecrated. As part of the consecration, he was required to swear allegiance to the King of England. With his loyalties now to the United States, Seabury turned to the Scottish Episcopal Church (not the recognized church) where he was consecrated as a Bishop in 1785. Upon return to the United States, his consecration was affirmed making him the first American Bishop.

Bishop Seabury was instrumental in the development of the Anglican liturgy in North America. It was based upon the Scottish Book of Common Prayer rather than the English version. He also was a proponent of a celebration of the Eucharist weekly rather than on occasion which was the tradition in Protestant churches following the reformation.

St. Columba was an Irish missionary who spread Christianity throughout Scotland and is known as one of the "Twelve Apostles of Ireland."

Around 560 A.D., he became embroiled in a controversy with St. Finnian of Movilla over a psalter which he had copied. St. Finnian of Movilla disputed his right to keep the copy leading to the Battle of Cul Dreimhne (Cooldrevny) in 561 A.D. in which hundreds of men died. Later that same year, a dispute with King Diarmait led him to induce the clan Neill to battle the King at Cooldrevny. Under the threat of excommunication, he chose to go into exile where he was determined to win for Christ as many souls as had been lost at the Battle of Cuil Dreimhne.

Leaving Ireland, St. Columba settled on the Island of Iona, a part of Scotland, where he founded a monastery. He was very active in establishing churches in Scotland and turned his monastery at Iona into a school for missionaries. St. Columba was also active in local politics and is credited with being a peace-maker among feuding groups.

St. Augustine of Canterbury was chosen by Pope Gregory the Great to convert the Anglo Saxons of southeastern England to Christianity. At Canterbury, St.

Augustine of Canterbury converted the King AEthelberht of Kent, a pagan, who gave him permission to convert his subjects. On Christmas Day, 564 A.D., St. Augustine baptized thousands. He was consecrated as a bishop by St. Virgilius at Arles. St. Augustine established Christ Church, Canterbury and also the monastery of St. Peter & St. Paul which after his death was renamed St. Augustine. He is considered the "Apostle to the English" and the founder of the English church.

Thomas Cranmer was a leader of the English Reformation and the Archbishop of Canterbury. Educated at Jesus College, Cambridge, he was ordained in 1520 and received a Doctorate of Divinity in 1526. He served under King Henry VIII, King Edward VI and Queen Mary I.

While at Cambridge, Cranmer helped to build the case for the annulment of King Henry VIII's marriage to Catherine of Aragon. When Arthur, Henry's brother and successor to the throne, died, his father, King Henry VII betrothed Arthur's widow to the future king raising biblical questions about marriage to a brother's wife. Cranmer also supported the principle of Royal Supremacy in which the king was considered sovereign over all in his kingdom.

Cranmer was appointed Archbishop of Canterbury in 1532 by King Henry VIII. One of his first acts as Archbishop of Canterbury was the "trial" for the annulment of King Henry VIII's marriage to Catherine of Aragon, in which he ruled that the marriage was against the law of God. Henry VIII had already secretly married Anne Boleyn who was pregnant. Shortly after the annulment, Cranmer married King Henry VIII and Anne Boleyn and crowned her queen.

Under King Edward VI, Cranmer made major changes to the Church of England. With English rather than Latin being the primary language of services in the English church, there was a need for a new prayer book. Cranmer wrote the first two versions of the Book of Common Prayer. With the assistance of other reformers on the Continent, he also made changes to the Eucharist, clerical celibacy, the role of images in places of worship, and the veneration of saints. Clerical celibacy was of particular interest to Cranmer since he had married while he was a priest.

When Queen Mary, a Roman Catholic, took the throne, Cranmer was tried and convicted of treason and heresy. He was imprisoned for over two years and later was burned at the stake.

Archbishop of Canterbury William Laud was a very controversial figure in England during a period of great turmoil. In 1625, King Charles I ascended to the throne. King Charles I wanted complete control and dissolved Parliament several times, including once for eleven years. One of his political allies was Archbishop Laud who preached that King Charles had the God-given right to rule, by Divine Right. By 1628, his position had hardened and he proclaimed that if you didn't support King Charles I and his policies, you weren't a good Christian. Archbishop Laud and other advisors persecuted the Puritans and tried to force the Presbyterian Scots to adapt the English Book of Common Prayer. The Reformers thought that King Charles I and Laud were trying to re-establish the Roman Catholic Church in England. King Charles I's fight with Parliament resulted in the English Civil War. Archbishop Laud was arrested in 1640 for treason, and was executed in 1645.

Bishop of London Henry Compton found himself in conflict with King James II, a Roman Catholic, and Compton was among those who encouraged William of Orange to overthrow King James II. Bishop Compton presided at the coronation of King William and Queen Mary.

Compton was very involved with the English colonies as a member of the Council of Trade and Plantations which had control over the colonies. He issued directions to the colonial governors that the churches operate in accordance with English instruction, increased the authority of the ministers in their parishes, and instructed the parishes to provide better compensation to the clergy. Compton also mandated that any ministers serving in the colonies had to have a certificate issued by him.

Compton was given a large land grant in the colonies. Although he never came to America, his son, John Compton, did. Henry Compton was instrumental in establishing the Anglican Church in Maryland, a state that had been founded as a Roman Catholic colony.

Bishop William White, born in Philadelphia, Pennsylvania, traveled to England for his ordination and again for his consecration as the second Bishop of Pennsylvania. Although White swore allegiance to the King as part of his consecration as Bishop, he supported the American Revolution. White was one of the leaders of the Anglican Church in America and he worked tirelessly on the relationship with the Church of England after American Independence. He served as Chaplain to the Continental Congress from 1778-1789, and as Chaplain of the Senate. He was the Episcopal Church's first and fourth Presiding Bishop.

He wrote a pamphlet which became a foundation for the Episcopal Church. Among his proposals was to have lay people participate in the governance of the church. When the first General Convention met in 1785, it was composed of both clergy and lay people.

He was known for his charitable works and participation in the life of the community. He was one of the citizens to urge the Pennsylvania legislature to fund what is now the Pennsylvania School for the Deaf, and served as its president for sixteen years. He was also a trustee of the University of Pennsylvania. He is credited with founding a school in Philadelphia for African American and Native American children and was active in prison ministry in Philadelphia.

Reverend James Madison was the first Bishop of Virginia. When Virginia declared its independence from England, the Virginia Convention, which governed both the Commonwealth as well as the Church of Virginia, ordered that the prayers for the King and England cease. In May 1785, sixty-nine parishes were represented at the first Diocesan Convention held in Richmond. The Reverend James Madison, rector of James City Parish and president of the College of William and Mary, was elected as President of the convention.

After the Revolutionary War, the Diocese of Virginia was one of the nine Dioceses represented at the first General Convention of the Episcopal Church in 1785. In 1786, the Reverend David Griffith was elected the Bishop for the Diocese of Virginia, but was unable to raise funds to travel to England for his consecration. In 1790, the Diocese of Virginia elected the Reverend James Madison as Bishop and he was consecrated in 1790 at Canterbury Cathedral.

Reredos in the Selden Chapel

St. Hilda was the founder of Whitby Abbey in England. She was born into the Deiran royal household, her father died when she was an infant and she was raised in the household of her uncle, Edwin of Northumbria. On Easter Day, 627 A.D., she was baptized at a small church on the site of the current York Minster. At age thirty-three, she answered a call to live as a nun where she learned the traditions of Celtic monasticism and was appointed the second Abbeyess of Hartlepool Abbey. At age forty-three, she founded

Whitby Abbey. The Abbey was a double monastery of both monks and nuns where men and women lived separately but worshiped in the same church.

St. Elizabeth was the mother of John the Baptist. She is the woman in the Biblical story who was barren but conceived a child at a very old age, that child being John the Baptist. John is portrayed with his mother at age twelve in the statue. John, of course, baptized Jesus in the River Jordan.

St. Monica was the mother of St. Augustine of Hippo whose life is commemorated with a statue on the main altar. Her life was interwoven with that of her son. He lived a hedonistic lifestyle, during which his mother prayed for him continually. Secretly, she followed him to Rome and Milan and and they were reconciled when he was baptized into the Christian faith, after having rejected it earlier. She is remembered for her suffering caused by her husband's violent temper and adultery, and for her prayerful life for her son's reformation.

Pocohantas was the daughter of Powhatan. Known by her Indian name, Matoaka, she was captured by the English during the Anglo-Indian hostilities of 1613 and was held for ransom. When she was released, she chose to stay with the English and converted to Christianity being baptized by the Reverend Alexander Whitaker and taking the English name of Rebecca. A painting of this event hangs in the rotunda of the United States Capitol. In 1614, she married John Rolfe. John, Rebecca and their son, Thomas, traveled to England in 1616. Upon the return trip to America, she died at Gravesend, England where she was buried.

St. Perpetua is to the left of the Selden Chapel reredos. She was born into a wealthy Roman family and converted to Christianity. She and a slave, Felicity, were arrested for their faith. After a period of imprisonment during which Perpetua's father begged her on several occasions to renounce her faith, she was taken to the amphitheater in Carthage. She was beaten with a scourge (a type of whip), then along with Felicity was thrown to a wild cow. When that failed to kill Perpetua, she was beheaded.

St. Blandina is to the right of the Selden Chapel reredos. She was a slave to a Christian in Lyon, France. She and her owner were both were imprisoned for their Christian faith and when they failed to renounce their faith, they were condemned to die. Emperor Marcus Aurelius allowed those who were Roman citizens to be executed by beheading but those who were not Roman citizens were to be tortured. St. Blandina was taken, along with some of the other prisoners, to the amphitheater in Lyon. There she was tied to a stake but the wild beasts would not touch her. She was then scourged, burned with a hot iron, and finally tied in a net and thrown to a wild bull who tossed her in the air. When those attempts were unsuccessful, St. Blandina was stabbed to death with a dagger.

Church banner

In 1976, a Christ & St. Luke's church banner was designed. It has a winged ox and a lamb. The winged ox

 is traditionally a symbol associated with St. Luke connoting sacrifice, service and strength. The lamb is, of course, a symbol of Jesus Christ. The colors on the banner, gold, white, red and blue, have traditionally signified royalty (gold), purity (white), and martyrdom (red). Set on a blue background, the banner has a cross, a sign of the passion of Christ and His resurrection.

⌖